Theory of Deductive Systems and Its Applications

MIT Press Series in the Foundations of Computing
Michael Garey, editor

Complexity Issues in VLSI: Optimal Layouts for the Shuffle-Exchange Graph and Other Networks, by Frank Thomson Leighton, 1983.

Equational Logic as a Programming Language, by Michael J. O'Donnell, 1985.

Theory of Deductive Systems and Its Applications, by S. Yu. Maslov, 1987.

Theory of Deductive Systems and Its Applications

S. Yu. Maslov

translated by
Michael Gelfond
and
Vladimir Lifschitz

The MIT Press
Cambridge, Massachusetts
London, England

7344-5149

MATH-STAT.

First published in the Soviet Union under the title *Teoriya deduktivnykh system i yeyo primeneniya.* © 1986 by Radio i Svyaz', Moscow.

This book was set in Times New Roman by Asco Trade Typesetting Ltd., Hong Kong, and printed and bound by Halliday Lithograph in the United States of America.

Library of Congress Cataloging-in-Publication Data

Maslov, S. I͡U. (Sergeĭ I͡Ur'evich)
  Theory of deductive systems and its applications.

  (MIT Press series in the foundations of computing)
  1. Logic, Symbolic and mathematical.   2. Algorithms.   3. Machine theory.
4. Artificial intelligence.   I. Title.   II. Series.
QA9.M34413   1987   511.3   86-21089
ISBN 0-262-13223-0 (Hardcover)

Contents

QA9
M 344131
1987
MATH

Series Foreword

Theoretical computer science has now undergone several decades of development. The "classical" topics of automata theory, formal languages, and computational complexity have become firmly established, and their importance to other theoretical work and to practice is widely recognized. Stimulated by technological advances, theoreticians have been rapidly expanding the areas under study, and the time delay between theoretical progress and its practical impact has been decreasing dramatically. Much publicity has been given recently to breakthroughs in cryptography and linear programming, and steady progress is being made on programming language semantics, computational geometry, and efficient data structures. Newer, more speculative, areas of study include relational databases, VLSI theory, and parallel and distributed computation. As this list of topics continues expanding, it is becoming more and more difficult to stay abreast of the progress that is being made and increasingly important that the most significant work be distilled and communicated in a manner that will facilitate further research and application of this work. By publishing comprehensive books and specialized monographs on the theoretical aspects of computer science, the series on Foundations of Computing provides a forum in which important research topics can be presented in their entirety and placed in perspective for researchers, students, and practitioners alike.

Michael R. Garey

Foreword

This is a book about modern methods and results of the general theory of deductive systems. Logical calculi, such as predicate calculus, were the first examples of completely formalized deductive systems. When the possibility of studying calculi as mathematical objects was understood, it became clear that the traditional "classical logic" was not the only possible logic, that other methods of reasoning, other deductive means, also "have the right to exist." A fundamental theoretical generalization of methods for the precise specification of logical and mathematical languages, the concept of a canonical calculus, has been introduced by the American mathematician E. L. Post.

The main thrust of this book is the idea that general calculi are promising as a tool for applications to areas outside mathematics. The book discusses the possibility of applying deductive systems to sciences that are only now beginning to use mathematical methods, in particular, sciences about mankind and about human culture, to the study of human interaction with the computer, and to the creation of artificial intelligence systems.

Maslov's interest in the areas of knowledge with nonformalized deductive methods led him to concentrate on the analysis of the process of selecting deductive systems whose application, conscious or unconscious, constitutes an essential part of culture.

A special place in the book is given to the theory of derivation search. Problems of this theory include determining the structure of possible derivations of a given hypothesis, constructing the best derivation, and estimating the time required for the search. The problems introduce time and dynamics into the theory of deductive systems. The systematic restructuring of the calculus and its improvement are essential features of this dynamics. Without such restructuring, proof search is helpless in nontrivial systems. So far as the mechanical realization of a fixed algorithm is concerned, the capabilities of the modern computer far exceed the possibilities of a human, but the ability to improve calculi remains so far a uniquely human one.

This book consists of three parts. In part I the mathematical apparatus of the theory of deductive systems is introduced and illustrated by many examples and the relation between deductive systems and algorithms is discussed. Deductive systems are characterized by the nonuniqueness of a possible way of their functioning. The concept of an algorithm, which is a model of discrete deterministic processes, is an important but special case of the concept of a deductive system. The concepts of a probabilistic canonical calculus (a calculus with a probability measure defined on the set of derivations) and of deductive information, important for the rest of the book, are also introduced in part I. The use of calculi for modeling specific (in particular, evolutionary) processes of transmitting information is discussed in part II. Part III gives a survey of the main results of the theory of derivation search and of the possibilities of its application.

Untimely death prevented Maslov from completing the work on the manuscript. He had planned to rewrite chapter 8, which is technically the most difficult; chapter 9 was not written at all. The author's last papers reflect, to some degree, his plans, so that their material is partially included in chapter 9.

The idea of writing a book on deductive systems for a wide audience was suggested to Maslov by V. V. Ivanov, who also interested him in applications to humanities. The author's friend and colleague, G. E. Mints, took it on himself to prepare the manuscript for publication in the Soviet Union. His help was so essential that this book could not have been published without it. The manuscript was carefully read by A. V. Gladky, and his remarks and suggestions cannot be overestimated. Effective support in publishing the book was given by Academicians G. S. Pospelov and O. M. Belotserkovsky.

Nina B. Maslov, D.Sc.

Theory of Deductive Systems and Its Applications

1 Rules of the Game

These rules, the sign language and grammar of the Game, constitute a kind of highly developed secret language drawing upon several sciences and arts ... which is capable of expressing and establishing interrelationships between the content and conclusions of nearly all scholarly disciplines.

Herman Hesse, *The Glass Bead Game*

In this introductory chapter, in accordance with an old tradition, we explain what problems we will study in this book and why. We explain what a deductive system is; we show that the area of applications of deductive systems is extremely wide and discuss the nature of its future applications. We enter a world that encompasses almost all the universe.

1.1 What Is a Deductive System?

In science and in practical applications we often encounter systems that can be described as follows: There are a certain number of initial objects and a certain number of rules for generating new objects from the initial objects and from those already constructed. To put it another way: There are an initial position (state) and "rules of the game" (rules for transition from one state to another). A system of this kind is called a *deductive system*, or a *calculus*.

Given a calculus, we may be interested in the properties of objects that, in principle, can be constructed and also in other questions: finding the best (in a certain sense) method for constructing a given object; predicting which objects will actually have been constructed by a certain instant of time, that is, what states the system will have come to; recommending how to control the process of generation with the purpose of developing it in a desired direction, directing the game to victory, etc. In addition, problems arise as to how various calculi can be constructed: calculi with given properties; calculi that generate given sets or generate them in an optimal (in a certain sense) way; problems of comparing and transforming calculi, etc. This is why we need a general theory of deductive systems.

The simplest calculus can be presented by the following description of the set of natural numbers: The number 1 is taken to be the initial object, and the only construction rule consists in adding 1 to the previously constructed number. (It can be said that this deductive system was the first in the history of human culture: The axiom is "one notch"; the rule is, "One more notch may be added to the notches already made.")

Quite interesting calculi are associated with deriving theorems in a mathematical theory. We know that theorems are propositions that can be derived from the axioms of the theory by means of correct inferences, that is, by applying rules of logical deduction, such as the famous *modus ponens*:

$$\frac{A, \, A \to B}{B} \tag{1.1}$$

(given the propositions A and A *implies B*, one can derive B). These calculi of mathematical logic were the first examples of completely formalized deductive systems clearly recognized as such. In fact, the rise of mathematical logic, this important and ramified field of science, was the result of the realization of the fact that logical deductive systems can be studied as mathematical objects.

When calculi became the object of study in mathematical logic, it was realized that our familiar "classical" logic is not the only one possible, that other kinds of logic, other methods of deduction, are also possible and necessary. Logical calculi multiplied, for there can be different games and different rules. And only one step was to be taken to arrive at a general concept of a deductive system, where the rules do not necessarily have anything to do with rules of deduction, with the logic of reasoning. This step was taken by the American mathematician E. L. Post in his 1943 paper [1], which became the first classical work on the general theory of deductive systems.

A Digression on History

And, perhaps, more than one treasure, having passed grandchildren, will be inherited by their sons.
O. Mandelstam

There are times in the history of science when concrete knowledge is valued above everything else, when empiricism triumphs and abstract schemes are held in contempt. Then other periods come, when scientists are interested primarily in theoretical concepts and the task of growing a body of facts around these concepts is put aside. (These periodic changes in scientific style and fashion are an important component of the spiritual climate of a society, and important correlations can be found between different aspects of these changes.) In this respect, science changed drastically after World War II, leading to the creation of the theory of systems, cybernetics, and, in particular, the theory of deductive systems.

Here is what Ludwig von Bertalanffy [2] writes about the general theory of systems:

> The idea goes back some considerable time: I presented it first in 1937 . . . . However, at that time theory was in bad repute in biology, and I was afraid of what Gauss, the mathematician, called the "clamor of the Boeotians." So I left my drafts in the drawer, and it was only after the war that my first publications on the subject appeared. Then, however, something interesting and surprising happened. It turned out that a change in intellectual climate had taken place, making model building and abstract generalizations fashionable. Even more: quite a number of scientists had followed similar lines of thought. So general system theory, after all, was not isolated . . . but corresponded to a trend in modern thinking. (p. 90)

We see that Bertalanffy refers to the prewar climate in biology, but similar evidence comes from scientists who worked in other fields. Norbert Wiener [3] writes, for instance, about the idea of modern computers, which he proposed in 1940:

> [Vannevar Bush] had no very high opinion of the apparatus I had suggested, especially because I was not an engineer and had never put any two parts of it together. His estimate of any work which did not reach the level of actual construction was extremely low. The only satisfaction I can now get is that I was right something like ten years before the techniques to prove my ideas were developed. (p. 239)

An analysis of publications in cybernetics, game theory, etc. confirms Bertalanffy's picture: Ideas developed before and during the war started to make an impact on scientific climate only after the publications of the late 1940s.

The history of Post's work is quite characteristic in that respect, too. The discoveries he made long before 1943 were presented to the public with the hope that the atmosphere in mathematics was suitable for the publication of such abstract ideas (in mathematics! in this center of abstract thought!). Still his publication turned out to be premature; the paper possibly affected the intellectual climate, but it had been forgotten by the time the apparatus of deductive systems became applicable. A special type of Post's calculi, formal grammars, became the basis of the intensive development of mathematical linguistics in the second half of the 1950s and for a number of years researchers in that field did not mention Post's paper and sometimes rediscovered his results. Only in the 1960s and 1970s did Post's ideas win sufficient recognition. It seems to me, however, that even now the apparatus of deductive systems does not play the role it deserves in discrete mathematics and its applications.

Let us discuss a few examples in more detail. By analogy with the calculi of mathematical logic, the initial objects of any deductive system S are called the *axioms* of the calculus, and the rules for constructing new objects are called its *inference rules*. (Recall that the word "calculus" is for us synonymous with "deductive system.") A *derivation* in S is any list of objects such that each element of the list either is an axiom or is obtained from previous elements of the list by one of the rules of inference. About the elements of the list we say that they are *derivable* in S.

If Q is a word (string of letters) in a certain alphabet, then $[Q]^{\langle l \rangle}$ stands for Q repeated l times. If Q consists of just one letter, then we write simply $Q^{\langle l \rangle}$.

EXAMPLE 1   Consider the set M of words of the form

$$|^{\langle 2^{2^n} \rangle} \qquad (n = 0, 1, 2, \ldots)$$

(that is, the set of numbers 2^{2^n} in base 1 notation). Let us construct the calculus S with two axioms, $||$ and $|*|$, and two inference rules:

a. From a word of the form $P*Q$, derive $P|*QPP|$.
b. From words P and $P*Q$, derive Q.

The list

$$|*|, \quad ||*|^{\langle 4 \rangle}, \quad |^{\langle 3 \rangle}*|^{\langle 9 \rangle}, \quad |^{\langle 4 \rangle}*|^{\langle 16 \rangle}, \quad ||, \quad |^{\langle 4 \rangle}, \quad |^{\langle 16 \rangle} \qquad (1.2)$$

is a derivation in S. As a matter of fact, the first word, $|*|$, is an axiom; the second, third, fourth words in the list are each obtained from the previous word by rule a; the fifth word, $||$, is again an axiom; the sixth word is obtained from the fifth and second words by rule b; finally, the last word, $|^{\langle 16 \rangle}$, is obtained from the sixth and fourth words by rule b.

It is easy to see that all words from M and all words of the form

$$|^{\langle n \rangle}*|^{\langle n^2 \rangle} \qquad (n = 1, 2, \ldots) \qquad (R_n)$$

are derivable in S. (As a matter of fact, the word R_1, that is, $|*|$, is an axiom. If R_n has been derived, then we get $|^{\langle n+1 \rangle}*|^{\langle n^2 \rangle}|^{\langle n \rangle}|^{\langle n \rangle}|$, that is, $|^{\langle n+1 \rangle}*|^{\langle n^2+2n+1 \rangle}$, which is identical with R_{n+1}.)

It should be observed that the method of deriving "auxiliary objects" used in this example is technically important. We were interested in the set M, but we also had to use words containing the symbol $*$.

In many cases, it is convenient to represent derivations as *trees*, in which the "leaves" are axioms and the transitions to a lower node are done according to inference rules.

EXAMPLE 1 (continued)   Derivation (1.2) can be represented by the following tree, in which the rules of inference used are shown to the right of the horizontal bars.

$$
\cfrac{\cfrac{|*|}{||,||*|^{\langle4\rangle}}\text{(a)}}{|^{\langle4\rangle}}\text{(b)} \qquad
\cfrac{\cfrac{\cfrac{\cfrac{|*|}{||*|^{\langle4\rangle}}\text{(a)}}{|^{\langle3\rangle}*|^{\langle9\rangle}}\text{(a)}}{|^{\langle4\rangle}*|^{\langle16\rangle}}\text{(a)}}{|^{\langle16\rangle}}\text{(b)}
$$

EXAMPLE 2. CLASSICAL PROPOSITIONAL CALCULUS   Let us use a calculus to represent the set of *tautologies*, that is, propositions that are formed from elementary propositions by means of logical connectives and that are true because of their logical structure, no matter whether their elementary components are true or false (see, for instance [4, 5]). We use only two connectives: ⊃ ("implies") and ⌐ ("not"); "and," "or," and other connectives can be expressed in terms of these two. (Readers not familiar with logic symbols should not worry: They are used only as shorthand. You should remember only how to read them:

⌐A: "not A,"
($A \wedge B$): "A and B,"
($A \vee B$): "A or B,"
($A \supset B$): "A implies B,"
($A \equiv B$): "A is equivalent to B,"
∃xA: "there exists x such that A,"
∀xA: "for all x, A.")

The objects with which this calculus operates are *propositional formulas*, that is, expressions formed from a potentially infinite set of *propositional variables* $p_1, p_2, \ldots$ by following the rules

1. Any variable is a formula.
2. If F is a formula, then ⌐F is also a formula.
3. If F and G are formulas, then ($F \supset G$) is also a formula.

The *axioms* of a propositional calculus are:

A1. $(p_1 \supset (p_2 \supset p_1))$,
A2. $((p_1 \supset (p_2 \supset p_3)) \supset ((p_1 \supset p_2) \supset (p_1 \supset p_3)))$,
A3. $((\neg p_1 \supset \neg p_2) \supset ((\neg p_1 \supset p_2) \supset p_1))$,

where p_1, p_2, p_3 are fixed propositional variables. The rules of inference are
the *modus ponens* (expression (1.1)) and the *substitution rule*

$$\frac{F}{[F]_G^P}$$

($[F]_G^P$ denotes the result of replacing all occurrences of variable P in
formula F by formula G). The tree

$$\cfrac{\cfrac{\cfrac{\cfrac{A2}{A1, (p_1 \supset (p_2 \supset p_1)) \supset ((p_1 \supset p_2) \supset (p_1 \supset p_1))}}{((p_1 \supset p_2) \supset (p_1 \supset p_1))}}{A1, ((p_1 \supset (p_2 \supset p_1)) \supset (p_1 \supset p_1))}}{\cfrac{(p_1 \supset p_1)}{(G \supset G)}}$$

proves that for every propositional formula G the formula $(G \supset G)$ is
derivable in this calculus. Every formula derivable in this calculus is true
for all values of its variables and vice versa; every tautology is derivable
(this was proved by Post in 1921). This deductive system is one of the
simplest and most typical logical calculi.

Notice that the set of propositional formulas is itself an inductively generated set, and, in turn, its definition is based on the inductively generated
set of variables. It is easy to see from this example that a detailed description
of a logical or logicomathematical calculus must be based on a multilevel
construction built from simple deductive systems describing the language
whose well-formed expressions are the objects of the "topmost" calculus.
For logicomathematical calculi, the derivable objects of the "topmost"
calculus are often called its *theorems*; in example 2, the theorems are
tautologies, and the language for describing the objects, propositional
formulas, is not described by an explicitly constructed deductive system.
To illustrate this with a more complex language, consider example 3.

EXAMPLE 3. THE LANGUAGE OF ARITHMETICAL FORMULAS   Well-formed expressions in this language are words (strings of "letters") in the alphabet

$\{n, v, t, f, (,), |, +, \cdot, =, \wedge, \vee, \supset, \neg, \forall, \exists\}.$

By Q and Q' we denote words in this alphabet. The words of the form $n|^{\langle n \rangle}$, where $n = 0, 1, 2, \ldots$, are interpreted as natural numbers, and the words $v|^{\langle n \rangle}$ are interpreted as variables ranging over natural numbers. (We include 0 in the set of natural numbers.) Expressions tQ and fQ' are interpreted as propositions: "Q is an arithmetical term" and "Q' is an arithmetical formula." (Arithmetical terms are built from variables and natural numbers by means of addition and multiplication.) The calculus of well-formed arithmetical expressions consists of the axiom "n" and the rules

$$\frac{nQ}{n|Q}; \quad \frac{nQ}{vQ}; \quad \frac{nQ}{tnQ}; \quad \frac{vQ}{tvQ}; \quad \frac{tQ, tQ'}{t(Q + Q')}; \quad \frac{tQ, tQ'}{t(Q \cdot Q')}; \quad \frac{tQ, tQ'}{f(Q = Q')};$$

$$\frac{fQ, fQ'}{f(Q \wedge Q')}; \quad \frac{fQ, fQ'}{f(Q \vee Q')}; \quad \frac{fQ, fQ'}{f(Q \supset Q')}; \quad \frac{fQ}{f \neg Q}; \quad \frac{vQ, fQ'}{f\forall vQQ'}; \quad \frac{vQ, fQ'}{f\exists vQQ'}.$$

Here is an example of a derivation in this calculus:

n,   n|,   v,   v|,   n||,   n|||,   tv,   tv|,

tn|||,   t(n|||·v),   t(v·v),   t((v·v) + (n|||·v)),   f(((v·v) + (n|||·v)) = v|),

f∃v|(((v·v) + (n|||·v)) = v|),   f∀v∃v|(((v·v) + (n|||·v)) = v|).

The last word in this derivation encodes the formula, which in conventional notation is written $\forall x \exists y (x^2 + 3x = y)$. It is easy to build the "next level" calculus over the one described, which in this case is arithmetic (see, for example, [4, 5]). Rule (1.1), for instance, becomes

$$\frac{fA, fB, A, (A \rightarrow B)}{B}.$$

EXAMPLE 4   We describe a problem about cutting fabric, known from mathematical programming [6], by means of a deductive system. There are M_1 pieces of fabric, each, say, 1 meter long, and M_2 pieces 1.2 meters each. We would like to cut the pieces into parts of sizes 0.8, 0.6, and 0.3 meters. We can describe the possible states of the system by quintuples:

$$m_1, m_2, n_1, n_2, n_3,$$

where m_1 and m_2 are the number of remaining pieces of the first and the number of remaining pieces of the second type, respectively, and n_1, n_2, and n_3 represent the number of parts of one of the three required sizes that have been cut. The initial state is described by the quintuple M_1, M_2, 0, 0, 0, which is the axiom of the system; inference rules correspond to various ways of cutting:

$$\frac{x+1, y, z, u, v}{x, y, z+1, u, v}; \quad \frac{x+1, y, z, u, v}{x, y, z, u+1, v+1}; \quad \frac{x+1, y, z, u, v}{x, y, z, u, v+3};$$

$$\frac{x, y+1, z, u, v}{x, y, z+1, u, v+1}; \quad \frac{x, y+1, z, u, v}{x, y, z, u+2, v}; \quad \frac{x, y+1, z, u, v}{x, y, z, u+1, v+2};$$

$$\frac{x, y+1, z, u, v}{x, y, z, u, v+4}.$$

The sixth rule, for instance, corresponds to the cut

$$120 = 60 + 30 + 30.$$

This example illustrates the main idea of modeling a system by a calculus: The evolution of the system corresponds to deriving further states from the initial state by applying possibilities from a certain set (in this example, a set of technological possibilities). It is essential for the applicability of the apparatus of calculi that the "moves," the steps transforming the system from one state to another, be *discrete*.

The *nondeterminicity* of the process, the possibility for the system to function in various ways, is another important feature that makes it advisable to use the apparatus of calculi. The nondeterminicity of functioning is a characteristic feature of deductive systems. The concept of an *algorithm*, which models discrete deterministic processes, is an important but limited special case of deductive systems (the case when only one inference rule can be applied to every derivable object with a uniquely defined result).

In example 4, the nonuniqueness results from the possibility of making several different decisions about how to do the next cut. It would be unnatural to describe this nonuniqueness in probabilistic terms, which is usually done for modeling nondeterministic processes. In the next example, a probabilistic description is more natural.

EXAMPLE 5   Consider the unisexual evolution of an individual J; we try to describe the set of all possible evolutionary descendants of J. (We assume that any individual is completely determined by its genotype and that genotypes are words in a certain alphabet.) One evolutionary step consists in the birth of a new fertile mutant. We get a deductive system with the axiom J and with the rules of inference corresponding to various permissible mutations (that is, mutations that produce fertile individuals). Consider, for instance, the "evolution" of the word ab resulting from "mutations" of the following three types:

a. $\dfrac{P}{PP}$;

b. $\dfrac{PbabQ}{PbbQ}$;

c. $\dfrac{PabbQ}{PabQ}$.

(The duplication rule a is a model of *polyploidy*, the type of mutation well known in biology; rules b and c permit deleting one letter in an appropriate "context" and model the type of mutation known in biology as *deletion*). It is easy to see that every "genotype" of the form

$$ab^{\langle n_1 \rangle}ab^{\langle n_2 \rangle}\ldots ab^{\langle n_k \rangle}$$

($k > 0$; $n_1, n_2, \ldots, n_k > 0$) can result from this "evolution," but words with two consecutive a's cannot be derived. But in the "actual" evolution of ab some of its potential descendants might not come into being. Let us make some assumptions about the probabilities of possible derivations. Assume that the mutant resulting from rule b does not possess a high vital capacity. Then almost all evolutionary descendants of the axiom will satisfy the additional condition $n_i = 1$. If rule b is a "lethal" mutation (its result is not viable), then every derivable word has the form $[ab]^{\langle 2h \rangle}$ ($h = 1, 2, \ldots$).

The calculi of examples 4 and 5, despite their simplicity, clearly demonstrate the possibilities of the apparatus of deductive systems for modeling natural processes. The next example shows how the concept of a deductive system can provide a language for solving combinatorial problems that often emerge in applications.

EXAMPLE 6. THE TRACING PROBLEM   Consider an undirected graph with nonnegative numbers, "capacities," assigned to its edges. Suppose that a "tracing assignment" is given: a set of triples (A, B, a), where A, B are vertices of the graph and a is a nonnegative number (the "thickness of the wire" by which A and B should be connected). The graph, along with all this information, is the axiom of our calculus; its inference rules correspond to the following transformations:

1. If the graph has an edge $A_1 \xleftarrow{a} A_2$ and the tracing assignment contains a triple of the form (A_1, A_3, b), then the capacity a can be replaced by $a - b$, and the triple by (A_2, A_3, b).

2. Any triple of the form (A, A, a) can be deleted from the tracing assignment.

It is easy to see that, whenever the object with the empty tracing assignment is derived in the calculus, the derivation gives a method for tracing the given graph, that is, for laying wires in it.

Problems

1.   Define a propositional calculus in the spirit of example 3, that is, with the derivable objects represented by words in a finite alphabet.

2.   The *length* of a linear derivation, or of a derivation tree, is the number of derivable objects in it. Determine what relationship exists between the lengths of linear derivations and the lengths of derivation trees with the same last word.

3.   Take a graph with a tracing assignment, construct the corresponding calculus, and derive the graph with the empty tracing assignment.

1.2   Let's Discuss the Possibilities

The theory of deductive systems is a branch of mathematical logic. From its very birth mathematical logic has been directed toward nonmathematical applications. Boole, Frege, Hilbert, and Whitehead and Russell perceived mathematical logic as an "applied science"—applicable to logic, psychology, philosophy, and philosophy of mathematics. Peano seems to be the only one among the "founders" of the field who assumed that the formalization of reasoning, by itself, would contribute to establishing new mathematical facts. No wonder, then, that applications of logic to mathematics are not that numerous and that its main accomplishments are in the area of philosophy of mathematics and its foundations and also in the field that the founders of mathematical logic did not foresee—computer science.

There is no doubt that mathematical logic will continue to contribute to the areas of science whose mathematization started in the twentieth century or is expected only now: biology, psychology, economics, linguistics, sociology, the study of art, theoretical history, and philosophy. The theory of deductive systems will play an especially important part in these applications. The fundamental nature of the concept of calculus is apparent to some degree from the examples given. It is determined, in particular, by the following facts:

i. Many systems and processes are discrete and nondeterministic.
ii. The concept of calculus is closely connected with the concept of algorithm.
iii. The principle of deduction plays an important part in the organization of knowledge and in human culture in general.

I discuss briefly the first two observations; the third is discussed in section 1.3.

The theory of deductive systems provides a useful, sometimes indispensable mechanism for creating quantitative models of the nondeterministic processes that can be adequately represented as discrete. Examples related to the use of formal grammars in mathematical linguistics are well known; grammars have also been applied to constructing models of the growth of biological systems (games such as "Evolution" give a good idea about such models), to the study of folklore and systems of poetry (see, for instance, [8]), etc. There are many books devoted specifically to grammars and their applications, for example, [9, 10]. In this book, however, little attention is given to them. I give a detailed treatment of applications of the theory of deductive systems to economic systems (chapters 5 and 6) and to modeling evolutionary processes, in particular, to modeling biological macroevolution (chapter 7).

The precise definition of an algorithm and the study of problems connected with algorithmic undecidability and with the complexity of algorithms are among the most significant achievements of mathematics in the twentieth century. Calculi are more general than algorithms; for this reason some algorithmic problems can be stated more adequately in the language of deductive systems. On the other hand, the availability of the well-developed apparatus of the theory of algorithms sometimes allows us to prove useful theorems about properties of calculi without much difficulty. This is why problems concerning algorithmic properties of deductive systems accompany us throughout this book.

These observations stress the universality of deductive systems, the prospects of their applications to various fields. It can be expected that in the near future the language of calculi will become as natural and commonplace in new applications of discrete mathematics as, for instance, the language of graph theory is today.

But now we should remember that universality is not only an advantage. Let us talk about disadvantages.

The Quality That Has Not Turned into Quantity

Even a brief look at examples 4 through 6 shows that an actual description of more or less complex processes in the language of deductive systems may be extremely bulky. To some degree this is simply the price one pays for using inference rules of a rather standard form. For modeling systems of some special type, one can establish beforehand a large number of conventions and abbreviations; having agreed on them, one may be able to describe a specific system in a relatively compact way. But the possibility of such a compactification does not change the essential fact that a stepwise description of a discrete process is in reality complex and bulky, often too bulky.

EXAMPLE 4 (continued)   If we agree beforehand that it is cutting that we are going to formalize in the form of calculi, then it is not difficult to simplify the method of describing the rules of inference. For instance, instead of the sixth rule we could write something such as $m_2 \rightarrow n_1 + 2n_2$. We can go a long way with abbreviations such as this; in the final account all information about the contents of the calculus of example 4 is contained in a short and easily decoded word, for example,

$$M_1 \cdot 100 + M_2 \cdot 120 \rightarrow 80, 60, 30.$$

It is more essential that, whenever a cutting problem is stated in a natural way (if, for instance, it is required that the number of sets of pieces be maximized), the order in which the methods of cutting are applied is irrelevant. The final result is not affected by changing the order of cuts, so that the "microtrajectory" of the system is not important. We can solve the problem on the "macrolevel," as it is done in mathematical programming. This is, of course, much more compact.

To put it differently, sometimes we do not need a "local" description of the behavior of the system, and we can restrict our attention to the "global" one. This is possible when some "homogeneities" (or "symmetries") are present that enable us to predict the macrobehavior of the system without knowing specific trajectories. In my example the homogeneity is connected with the permutability of cuts and with the fact that the materials as well as the products are identical. But, if the result depends strongly on the state of the system at a given moment of time (and that happens in the cases most interesting from the viewpoint of applications of calculi), then the local description of the system is at the heart of the matter.

Thus the large size of descriptions using calculi can be somewhat reduced, but it cannot be completely eliminated. It is a fortunate circumstance, then, that there exists the possibility of using computers, which are so well suited for modeling discrete (and, when some technical difficulties are overcome, nondeterministic) processes. This is a sharp difference between computers and humans, who can work with "global" pictures much more easily. I come back to this distinction later. The perspectives of interaction between humans and computers form the background of this book and partially the contents of part III.

I should mention one more specific difficulty connected with the universality of the language of calculi. As we will see, arbitrarily complex calculi can be constructed from inference rules of extremely simple structure. Such inference rules are much simpler than the rules actually needed in applications, whereas the complexity of the calculi that can be formed from them is much greater than the complexity of the calculi that occur in applications. This creates practically (and, perhaps, theoretically) insurmountable difficulties in drawing the boundary between "really needed" and "unreal," too complex, algorithmically undecidable systems. This leads to natural though exaggerated skepticism concerning the applicability of the classical apparatus of the theory of algorithms and deductive systems.

The large size of real systems and the robustness of some of the methods used (for example, studying algorithmic undecidability instead of algorithmic complexity) imply that almost all applications of the theory of deductive systems are related to simple models. Almost always we are concerned with the qualitative modeling of processes rather than with computing their numerical characteristics.

1.3   The Tower of Deductive Systems

Then they said, "Come, let us build ourselves a city, and a tower with its top in the heavens...." And the Lord said, "Behold, they are one people, and they have all one language; and this is only the beginning of what they will do; and nothing that they propose to do will now be impossible for them."
Genesis 11:4–6

The role of deduction in constructing scientific theories is well known. This applies both to mathematics, whose deductive structure admits an adequate formalization in terms of modern mathematical and logical calculi (at least in principle and with few exceptions), and to other sciences, with much less formalized deductive means. The apparatus of calculi not only grasps the linguistic (or *syntactic*) side of the cognitive process but also provides forms of reasoning, "rules of the intellectual game," which people follow when they state the results of their thoughts, argue that their opinions are true and valid, or persuade their opponents.

Examples 2 and 3 give simple illustrations, but overall the process of conscious and unconscious application of calculi embraces cognition in general and leads logicians to constructing, say, a "logic of quantum physics" [11] and leads humanists, enchanted in their childhood by Euclidean geometry, to constructing "deductive ethics," in which assertions such as "He likes to work, so he is a good person" become theorems.

It is especially important that deductive systems not only can be used for the purpose of formally stating the results of thought processes but can also serve as a means of analysis of the thought processes themselves. As a matter of fact, a theory of derivation search can be developed, which leads us to the discovery of some mechanisms of creativity. (Wide classes of problems requiring creative work can be represented naturally as problems of finding derivations in certain specially selected deductive systems.) This theory opens a slot through which we can "look into the head" of, say, a mathematician or a chess player, look even at the unconscious parts of the creative process. The theory of derivation search is closely connected with the psychology of creativity and the automation of scientific research, with the design of efficient search algorithms, and with constructing artificial intelligence systems. Problems of this sort are discussed in part III. There we encounter the situation in which the essence of the process that is being modeled is the transition from one calculus to another.

Thus a calculus provides a "theory" of the given field, a method of the fixation of knowledge about methods of solving problems of a given type that are available at a certain point in time. Accordingly, the process of development of the field consists of two types of stages: stages of work inside a fixed deductive system and stages when the system itself is being created or modified. Because these stages repeatedly give rise to each other, a "tower" of calculi, in a manner of speaking, comes into being. Its ground floor is occupied by data about the outside world, and transition to every next level is performed on the basis of the data produced by systems on lower levels.

If we understand the terminology broadly ("the language of culture" and "artistic canon" are similar in many respects to the concept of calculus), then what has been said applies to various cognitive methods: scientific, technological, artistic. This determines the structure of this book: modeling processes by means of calculi is discussed in part II, and ascent to calculi of higher levels in part III. Part I is devoted to the study of calculi per se; it gives the necessary mathematical background.

The greater part of this book can be understood by readers without knowledge of mathematics beyond the high school level. Those readers interested specifically in applications to economics, biology, or psychology can read part I and then proceed directly to chapters 5 and 6, to chapter 7, or to chapters 8 and 9, respectively.

To master completely all the material, including the problems, serious work, certain mathematical culture, and, of course, interest in mathematical aspects of the theory are required. On the other hand, readers who have mastered all this material are already familiar with the state of the art and are ready to conduct original research.

Now we can take a walk in the world of deductive systems, start the storm of the tower. Happy journey!

I Mathematics of Calculi

2 Post's Canonical Systems

Deductive systems can be designed for deriving objects of various forms. But it is essential that each derivable object be finite, or, more precisely, *contain a finite amount of information.* It can be assumed that the objects under consideration can always be encoded (without loss of "information," whatever this word means) by a finite sequence of symbols (*letters*), each symbol being an element of a finite set (*alphabet*) specified beforehand. It is also essential that each letter, by itself, carry no "information" except that it is possible to distinguish it from other letters in the alphabet; it can be replaced by any other symbol, provided that this possibility is not lost.

2.1 How to Construct All That Can Be Constructed

The objects under consideration are *words* in finite alphabets. Calculi with finite objects but infinite alphabets, which occur quite often, can easily be modified by replacing their letters with appropriate words (as propositional variables in example 2 are replaced with words $v|^{\langle i \rangle}$ in example 3 (chapter 1). At this point let me digress and make two remarks.

The Art of Calligraphy

An example of calligraphy shows that a written word may contain much more "information" than the same word typed (or written sloppily). The aesthetic impression disappears when the shape of the characters is changed; the very decomposition of a word into letters is inadequate for the essence of calligraphy. Quasi-paradoxes of information happen every time the artistic aspect is combined with the formal, semantic one. (Think of poetry written in hieroglyphics, of the essence of the language of any art.)

Remark 1   In a number of cases, of interest are deductive systems with infinitely long derivable objects. I do not use them in this book.

Remark 2   It is inconvenient to represent objects with two-dimensional or many-dimensional structures by words, that is, by linear objects. Readers can easily see this if they try to do such an encoding for example 6. This fact should be taken into account in connection with the problems of complexity of deductive systems, but it is not essential for my present purposes.

A *canonical calculus* is a quadruple of the form

$$(\mathbf{A}, \mathbf{P}, A, \Pi), \tag{2.1}$$

where **A** and **P** are disjoint alphabets (**A** is called the *alphabet of calculus* (2.1), and the letters of **P** are called *variables* of the calculus); A is a list of axioms (that is, words in **A**), and Π is the list of *inference rules*, each rule being of the form

$$
\begin{array}{c}
\Sigma_1 \\
\vdots \\
\Sigma_m \\
\hline
\Sigma_0
\end{array}
\tag{2.2}
$$

$(m \geqslant 1)$, where Σ_i are words in the alphabet $\mathbf{A} \cup \mathbf{P}$, $i = 0, 1, 2, \ldots, m$, such that all variables from Σ_0 occur in the word $\Sigma_1 \ldots \Sigma_m$. $\Sigma_1, \ldots, \Sigma_m$ are called the *premises* of (2.2), and Σ_0 its *conclusion*. We say that expression (2.2) is an *m-premise rule*.

It remains to define when a word Q_0 is obtained from $Q_1, \ldots, Q_m$ by rule (2.2). Assign a word in **A** to every variable (that is, to a letter of **P**) that occurs in (2.2) (the *value* of that variable). If we now replace all variables in (2.2) with their values, then $\Sigma_0, \ldots, \Sigma_m$ become words in **A**. If for some choice of values of variables this process transforms Σ_i into Q_i ($i = 0, \ldots, m$), then we say that Q_0 is *immediately derivable* from $Q_1, \ldots, Q_m$ by rule (2.2). This is expressed by $Q_1, \ldots, Q_m \vdash Q_0$; accordingly, we sometimes write rule (2.2) in the form

$$\Sigma_1, \ldots, \Sigma_m \vdash \Sigma_0.$$

EXAMPLE 1 (continued from chapter 1)   The deductive system constructed in example 1 can be described as a canonical calculus, that is, in the form (2.1):

$$
\mathbf{A} = \{|, *\}, \quad \mathbf{P} = \{p, q\}, \quad A = \{|*|, \|\}, \quad \Pi = \left\{ \frac{p*q}{p|*qpp|}, \quad \frac{p*q}{q} \quad \frac{p}{q} \right\}.
$$

The new notation does not change, of course, the set of formulas derivable in the calculus or the set of derivations; in particular,

$$|^{\langle 4 \rangle} * |^{\langle 16 \rangle}, \ |^{\langle 4 \rangle} \vdash |^{\langle 16 \rangle},$$

which can be verified by substituting $|^{\langle 4 \rangle}$ for p and $|^{\langle 16 \rangle}$ for q in the second rule of Π.

Notice that the relation of immediate derivability may also apply to words not derivable in the calculus. For instance, if in the first (one-premise) rule of Π we select $|$ as the value of p and $\|$ as the value of q, then we get $|*\|$ in the premise and $\|*|^{\langle 5 \rangle}$ in the conclusion. Thus $|*\| \vdash \|*|^{\langle 5 \rangle}$, even though neither word, as we know, is derivable in the calculus (because they do not have the form $|^{\langle n \rangle}*|^{\langle n^2 \rangle}$).

Recursively Enumerable Sets

If the alphabet of a calculus contains $\mathbf{A}$, then we say that this is a calculus *over* $\mathbf{A}$; two calculi over $\mathbf{A}$ are *equivalent relative to* $\mathbf{A}$ if any word in $\mathbf{A}$ that is derivable in one calculus is derivable in the other. We say that a pair

$$(\mathbf{A}, K), \tag{2.3}$$

where K is a canonical calculus over $\mathbf{A}$, is a *representation* of (or that it *represents*) the sets of words in $\mathbf{A}$ that are derivable in K. Here $\mathbf{A}$ is called the *main alphabet* of the representation, and the complement of $\mathbf{A}$ relative to the full alphabet of K is called the *auxiliary alphabet*. K *strictly represents* the set of all words derivable in it.

We say that a set M of words in $\mathbf{A}$ is *recursively enumerable* (abbreviated r.e.) if there exists a representation (2.3) for it (that is, if it can be represented by a calculus in which, in addition to the words from M, some other words may be derivable, *but* these additional words must contain letters from the auxiliary alphabet). For example, the calculus of example 1, with $\{|\}$ selected as the main alphabet, demonstrates the recursive enumerability of the set

$$\{\|, |^{\langle 4 \rangle}, \ldots, |^{\langle 2^{2^n} \rangle}, \ldots\}. \tag{2.4}$$

The process of enumeration, or generation, of a set M represented by a calculus K can be conveniently described in terms of a *derivation algorithm* for K. (Algorithms in general are discussed in chapter 3.) The simplest derivation algorithm is derivation "by brute force." In the first step it generates all axioms of K (there is a finite number of them), and in each step thereafter it generates all words immediately derivable (that is, derivable by one application of an inference rule) from the words generated before. When applied to a word P, the algorithm stops when P is derived. By that time, a derivation of P will have been generated as well.

Let us prove that *the union and intersection of two r.e. sets are r.e.* Let $(\mathbf{A}, K_1)$ and $(\mathbf{A}, K_2)$ be representations of M_1, M_2, where $K_1 = (\mathbf{A}_1, \mathbf{P}_1, A_1, \Pi_1)$ and $K_2 = (\mathbf{A}_2, \mathbf{P}_2, A_2, \Pi_2)$. Let ξ_1 and ξ_2 be distinct letters not belonging to $\mathbf{A}_1 \cup \mathbf{A}_2$. Let ${}^{\xi_1}\!A_1$ be the result of appending ξ_1 to the beginning of each axiom from A_1. Similarly, ${}^{\xi_1}\Pi_1$ is obtained by appending ξ_1 to the beginning of each premise and the conclusion of each rule from Π_1. The meanings of ${}^{\xi_2}\mathbf{A}_2$ and ${}^{\xi_2}\Pi_2$ are similar. Now construct the calculus $K^{\cup}$ with the alphabet $\mathbf{A}_1 \cup \mathbf{A}_2 \cup \{\xi_1, \xi_2\}$, the alphabet of variables $\mathbf{P}_1 \cup \mathbf{P}_2$, the axioms ${}^{\xi_1}\!A_1 \cup {}^{\xi_2}\!A_2$ and the rules

$$ {}^{\xi_1}\Pi_1 \cup {}^{\xi_2}\Pi_2 \cup \{\xi_1 p \vdash p, \xi_2 p \vdash p\} $$

(here $p \in \mathbf{P}_1 \cup \mathbf{P}_2$). The reader can easily verify that $(\mathbf{A}, K^{\cup})$ represents $M_1 \cup M_2$.

Thus, for constructing the union, we essentially combine the deductive capabilities of K_1 and K_2. Perhaps, for constructing the intersection we should take the intersection of these capabilities? No! the insightful reader will object with indignation. Calculus $K^{\cap}$ should be constructed in exactly the same way as $K^{\cup}$, only with the last two inference rules replaced with one two-premise rule, $\xi_1 p, \xi_2 p \vdash p$.

The reader is quite right. And, while I am at it, the reader can also think about whether the union $M_1 \cup M_2$ can be represented simply by

$$ (\mathbf{A}, (\mathbf{A}_1 \cup \mathbf{A}_2, \mathbf{P}_1 \cup \mathbf{P}_2, A_1 \cup A_2, \Pi_1 \cup \Pi_2)). $$

There are serious reasons to believe that *any set that can be generated or enumerated by any constructive means is r.e.* At any rate, during the time that mathematics has been in existence, no method for generating sets has been invented that offers a finite number of quite definite actions for generating each element and that leads to a set which is not r.e. There are many different approaches to defining a constructively generated set, based on seemingly different concepts of an algorithm. And all these approaches lead to the same class of sets! The apparatus of canonical calculi is sufficiently powerful to model the work of all algorithms and all deductive systems. (In chapter 3 I discuss this fact in more detail.) The claim about the universality of the apparatus of canonical calculi is mathematically equivalent to the *Church-Turing thesis*, famous in the theory of algorithms; detailed arguments in favor of this thesis can be found in almost any book on the theory of algorithms (for example, [12, 13]).

To feel the difference between constructive and nonconstructive descriptions of sets, it is useful to try to generate the complement of a given r.e. set (that is, the complement with respect to the set of all words in the main alphabet). The complement of the set with representation $(\mathbf{A}, K)$ is a precisely described object. But this kind of description does not provide any sequence of actions that after a finite number of steps generates even one element of the complement. Sometimes, after studying K, we may be able to invent a calculus K^c corresponding to the complement, but there is no regular procedure that allows us to transform K into K^c (such as the procedures we used to transform K_1 and K_2 into $K^\cup$ and $K^\cap$). As a matter of fact, the complement operation may lead beyond the class of r.e. sets: An enumerable set can be constructed whose complement is not r.e. (see section 2.3).

Remark 3   The definition of r.e. sets allows the use of an auxiliary alphabet. The necessity of auxiliary letters can be reduced to a minimum but not eliminated altogether; even set (2.4) cannot be represented by a calculus in the alphabet $\{|\}$ (see problems 3 and 4), that is, cannot be strictly represented.

Problems

1.   Prove that the following sets of words are r.e.:
(a) $|^{\langle n^3 \rangle}$ $(n = 1, 2, 3, \ldots)$.
(b) $|^{\langle p \rangle}$ (p is a prime number).
(c) $a^{\langle n \rangle} b^{\langle 2^n \rangle}$ $(n = 2, 3, \ldots)$.
(d) Words in the alphabet $\{a, b\}$ having the form PP^T, where P is any word and P^T is P written backward.
(e) The complement of (2.4).

2.   Let M be an r.e. set of words in $\mathbf{A}$, and let $a \in \mathbf{A}$. Prove the recursive enumerability of the subsets of M consisting of words (a) not containing a, (b) containing exactly three occurrences of a.

3.   For every rule (2.2) one can specify an N such that the length of the conclusion of any application of the rule is at most Nl, where l is the greatest of the lengths of the premises of this application. Prove this, and prove that no calculus in the one-letter alphabet can represent rule (2.4).

4.   For any calculus over $\mathbf{A}$ construct a calculus in a one-letter extension (that is, in the alphabet $\mathbf{A} \cup \{\xi\}$, where ξ is a new letter) of $\mathbf{A}$ that is equivalent to it.

2.2   Deriving Derivations (Post's Reductions)

We believe that the apparatus of canonical calculi has all the capabilities needed for deriving arbitrarily complex (but constructively generated) sets.

But is it not possible that the same can be done with much more limited tools? Many important deductive systems have inference rules of a much more special form than rule (2.2). Can it be the case that such rules are still sufficient for representing arbitrary r.e. sets? This is important for studying special types of calculi, and in the rest of this chapter I discuss a few "specializations" of the apparatus of canonical calculi (which use more limited deductive tools but represent the same class of sets).

I investigate the specializations with which the theory of deductive systems started. (In particular, some basic results in this direction were obtained by Post [1]). One of the most fundamental and frequently used facts is that one-premise rules alone will do. More precisely, the following holds:

THEOREM (POST'S FIRST REDUCTION)   For every canonical calculus K, $K = (\mathbf{A}, \mathbf{P}, A, \Pi)$, one can construct a calculus K' equivalent to K with respect to $\mathbf{A}$ that has one axiom and only one-premise inference rules.

The idea of the proof is to extend $\mathbf{A}$ by adding a "separator" (for forming lists of words) and to construct a calculus whose derivable objects are "derivations" in the given calculus. For instance, take the symbol $\square$ ($\square \notin \mathbf{A}$), and add the letters p_1, p_2, p_3 to the alphabet P; for every axiom R from A introduce the rule

$$p_1 \square \vdash p_1 \square R \square, \qquad\qquad (2.5)$$

and for every rule (2.2) from Π introduce the one-premise rule

$$\frac{p_1 \square \Sigma_1 \square \ldots \square \Sigma_m \square}{p_1 \square \Sigma_1 \square \ldots \square \Sigma_m \square \Sigma_0 \square}. \qquad\qquad (2.6)$$

I also add the "permutation" and "word extraction" rules:

$$\frac{p_1 \square p_2 \square p_3 \square}{p_1 \square p_3 \square p_2 \square}, \quad \frac{p_1 \square p_2 \square}{p_2}.$$

Let us verify that every word derivable in K can be derived in the calculus I have constructed. The proof uses the method typical for the theory of calculi—*induction on the length of the derivation.*

Let $S_1, S_2, \ldots, S_n$ be a derivation in K. Let us prove that the word

$$\square [S_1 \square]^{\langle M \rangle} [S_2 \square]^{\langle M \rangle} \ldots [S_n \square]^{\langle M \rangle},$$

where M is the maximum number of premises of the rules in Π, is derivable in the constructed calculus. If $n = 1$, then S_n (that is, S_1) is an axiom of K, and $\Box[S_1\Box]^{\langle M\rangle}$ can be obtained by applying the appropriate rule (2.5) M times to the axiom $\Box$.

Assume that the assertion holds for derivations of length $n - 1$, and assume that

$$S_{i_1}, \ldots, S_{i_m} \vdash S_n$$

in K. Consider the word $\Box[S_1\Box]^{\langle M\rangle}\ldots[S_{n-1}\Box]^{\langle M\rangle}$, and for every j ($1 \leqslant j \leqslant m$) let us mark some occurrence S_{i_j} in that word (S_{i_j} should be an occurrence limited by the symbol $\Box$). This should be done in such a way that, whenever $S_{i_j} = S_{i_k}$ and $j \neq k$, different occurrences are marked. (Actually, the need to have a separate occurrence for each of coinciding premises causes the necessity of repeating each element of the given derivation M times.) Now the marked occurrences should be moved to the end of the word; that is, by applying the permutation rule M times, we should get a word of the form

$$p\Box S_{i_1}\Box\ldots\Box S_{i_m}\Box.$$

Now the application of rule (2.6) M times (in conjunction with the necessary permutations) completes the induction step.

The assertion proved by induction immediately implies that every word derivable in K is derivable in the constructed calculus as well (just apply the word extraction rule).

Unfortunately, if we tried to prove the converse—that every word in **A** derivable in the constructed calculus is derivable in the given one—we would fail. As a matter of fact, the calculus we constructed may not be equivalent to K, and its transparent design has to be corrected and made more complex. (Why the equivalence can be violated is clear from the complete proof of the theorem, which follows.)

Proof   As the alphabet of K' we take $\mathbf{A} \cup \{*, \Box\}$; its axiom is $*\Box$, and its inference rules, instead of those specified in the previous construction, are selected as follows (q and p with and without subscripts are new variables):

$$\frac{q\Sigma_1\ldots\Sigma_m*p\Box\Sigma_1\Box\ldots\Box\Sigma_m\Box}{q\Sigma_1\ldots\Sigma_m\Sigma_0*p\Box\Sigma_1\Box\ldots\Box\Sigma_m\Box\Sigma_0\Box},$$

$$\frac{q*p\Box}{qR*p\Box R\Box}, \quad \frac{q_1q_2q_3*p_1\Box p_2\Box p_3\Box}{q_1q_3q_2*p_1\Box p_3\Box p_2\Box}, \quad \frac{q_1p_2*p_1\Box p_2\Box}{p_2}. \tag{2.7}$$

LEMMA   Every word derivable in K' either is derivable in K or has the form

$$Q*\Box S_1 \Box \ldots \Box S_n \Box \qquad (n \geqslant 0), \tag{2.8}$$

where Q is a word in $\mathbf{A}$ and all words S_i are derivable in K.

In the proof we again use induction on the length of the derivation (in K'). The axiom of K' has the form (2.8) (Q is empty and $n = 0$).

The induction step takes a typical form: If $p \vdash p'$ and p satisfies the lemma, then so does p'. This is verified separately for each rule of K'. If, for instance, the rule of appending an axiom is applied, then the premise of this application must have the form (2.8); then the conclusion is

$$QR*\Box S_1 \Box \ldots \Box S_n \Box R \Box.$$

Adding occurrences of R preserves form (2.8) because R is a word in $\mathbf{A}$ and is derivable in K (it is an axiom of K). Similarly, the permutation rule does not add new letters to the left of $*$ or new words between the letters $\Box$ to the right of $*$. In a similar way, the last rule transforms a word of form (2.8) into S_n, which is derivable in K. Here we use the fact that, when this rule is applied, the value of p_2 must be a word in $\mathbf{A}$ (because p_2 also occurs to the left of $*$, where by the induction hypothesis only words in $\mathbf{A}$ can occur).

This last part of the proof explains why it was necessary to accumulate something to the left of $*$: The only goal was to ensure that the values of some of the necessary variables do not, by chance, contain $\Box$. If we look now at rule (2.7), we see that all variables from $\Sigma_0 \Sigma_1 \ldots \Sigma_m$ occur in the premise of this rule to the left of $*$ (recall that Σ_0 contains variables that occur only in $\Sigma_1 \ldots \Sigma_m$). Hence the application of rule (2.7) to form (2.8) necessarily corresponds to some immediate derivability in K of the form

$$S_{n-m+1}, \ldots, S_n \vdash S$$

and consequently does not lead outside of the class of words of form (2.8). The lemma is proved.

So derivability in K' implies derivability in K. The converse is proved exactly as in the previous section (because to the left of $*$ we can do exactly the same things as to the right, and the "right-hand side" of our K' is the calculus of the previous section).

Remark 4   In fact, K' can be constructed in such a way that the length of the derivation in K' of any word in $\mathbf{A}$ is the same as the length of the derivation of the same word in K.

So far I have discussed only Post's first reduction. The theorem I have proved can be made significantly stronger. Calculi with one axiom and inference rules of the form

$$Gp \vdash pG' \tag{2.9}$$

(here p is a variable and G and G' are words in the alphabet of the calculus) are called *normal*.

POST'S THEOREM   For every canonical calculus over $\mathbf{A}$ one can construct a normal calculus that is equivalent to it over $\mathbf{A}$.

To prove Post's theorem, we need three more reductions. The second of Post's reductions consists in the transition to a calculus whose rules have the form

$$G_1 p_1 \ldots p_k G_{k+1} \vdash G_1' p_1 \ldots p_k G_{k+1}' \qquad (k \geqslant 1), \tag{2.10}$$

where all the p_i are distinct variables and all the G_i are words in the alphabet of the calculus. Here, k may vary from one rule to another.

EXAMPLE 7   The idea of this reduction can be illustrated on the calculus

$$(\{|\}, \{p\}, \{|\}, \{p \vdash pp\}),$$

which represents the set of powers of 2 (that is, words of the form $|^{\langle 2^n \rangle}$, where $n = 1, 2, \ldots$). The reduction introduces a separate variable for each occurrence of the same variable in an inference rule; then the value of the variable is gradually "pumped" from the occurrences in the premises to the occurrences in the conclusion. In the example this is realized by the calculus in the alphabet $\{, |, \Box\}$ with the axiom $|\Box\Box$ and the rules

$$\frac{|p_1 \Box p_2 \Box p_3}{p_1 \Box | p_2 \Box | p_3}, \quad \frac{\Box p_2 \Box p_3}{p_2 p_3 \Box \Box}, \quad \frac{p_1 \Box \Box}{p_1}.$$

The words derivable in this calculus have the form $|^{\langle 2^n \rangle}$ or the form

$$|^{\langle k \rangle} \Box |^{\langle l \rangle} \Box |^{\langle l \rangle} \qquad (k + l = 2^n, n = 1, 2, \ldots).$$

The gradual decrease in the value of k and increase in the value of l correspond to the mentioned "pumping" of the value of p in the originally given calculus from the only occurrence in the premise to the two occurrences in the conclusion. The equivalence of these calculi with respect to $\{|\}$ is easily proved.

The technical implementation of this idea is rather bulky. The second reduction is the most difficult of Post's reductions.

A calculus obtained by the third reduction has rules of the same form (2.10) with the additional condition $k = 1$.

EXAMPLE 7 (continued)   Let us discuss the idea of the third reduction by using the example of the transformation of the rule

$$\frac{|p_1 \square p_2 \square p_3}{p_1 \square |p_2 \square |p_3}.$$

The operation of this rule is modeled by the gradual transfer of letters from the beginning of the word to its end with the replacement of encountered symbols $\square$ by the word $\square|$. To this end, a new letter $\#$ is introduced, and the new rules are written

$$\frac{|p}{\# p \#}, \quad \frac{\# |p}{\# p|}, \quad \frac{\# \square p}{\# p \square|}, \quad \frac{\# \# p}{p}.$$

Here again, carrying out the reduction in the general case is, of course, much more difficult.

Finally, Post's last reduction consists in the transition to a normal calculus.

EXAMPLE 7 (continued)   I could continue the work on modeling the rules that were just written out by rules of form (2.9). However, the idea of the fourth reduction can also be demonstrated if from the very beginning we use a somewhat different schema for generating the set in question. We can write the representation

$$(\{|\}, (\{|, T\}, \{p\}, \{|\}, \{|p \vdash pTT, Tp \vdash p|\}\}) \tag{2.11}$$

and remember that a normal calculus can be constructed effectively by using doubles for the letters of the original alphabet.

Problems

1.   Represent set (2.4) by a one-premise calculus.

2.   Prove the assertion from remark 4.

3.   Prove Post's theorem.

2.3   One for All

Turing built various automata: some of them made machines, others baked bread, still others calculated and could perform logical reasoning. He worked for forty years, until he invented an automaton which could do everything.
Stanislaw Lem

One of the most convincing proofs of the power of canonical calculi is given by the fact that a calculus can be constructed that models the work of absolutely all calculi at once. More precisely, I talk here about modeling all calculi in a fixed alphabet. We already know that we can confine ourselves to modeling normal calculi only: Even they are equivalent to arbitrary canonical calculi. (A more cumbersome construction of a universal calculus that does not require the preliminary transition to normal calculi can be found in [14].)

Consider a normal calculus

$$(\mathbf{A}, \{p\}, \{R\}, \{G_1 p \vdash p G_1', \ldots, G_n p \vdash p G_n'\}),$$

and let its *designation* be the following word in the alphabet $\mathbf{A} \cup \{\Box, \rightarrow, \models\}$:

$$R \Box G_1 \rightarrow G_1' \Box \ldots \Box G_n \rightarrow G_n' \Box \models.$$

For instance, $\Box \models$ is the designation of the calculus that has no inference rules and that has the null word as the only axiom; the word

$$|\Box| \rightarrow TT \Box T \rightarrow |\Box \models \tag{2.12}$$

designates normal calculus (2.11) from example 7. Let us now construct a calculus *universal for the normal calculi in* $\mathbf{A}$. (The rest of the exposition has much in common with the one proposed in [15]).

THEOREM (ON THE UNIVERSAL CALCULUS)   One can construct a canonical calculus $U^{\mathbf{A}}$ in the alphabet

$$\mathbf{A} \cup \{\Box, \rightarrow, \models\} \qquad (\mathbf{A} = \{a_1, \ldots, a_k\}), \tag{2.13}$$

such that a word is derivable in it if and only if it has the form NP, where N is the designation of some normal calculus in the alphabet $\mathbf{A}$ and P is a word derivable in that calculus.

Remark 5   It turns out that even such a complex set can be represented strictly (that is, without extending alphabet (2.13)), even though a strict representation is impossible for the simple set from example 1!

We take the word $\Box\models$ to be the only axiom of U^A, and its inference rules are ($p, p_1, p_2, q, q_1, q_2, r$ are the variables of U^A):

1.

$$\frac{p\Box\models p}{pa_i\Box\models pa_i} \quad (i = 1, \ldots, k)$$

(the rules to be used in the absence of rules),

2.

$$\frac{\begin{array}{c} p_1 p_2 \Box\models p_1 p_2 \\ q\models r \end{array}}{q p_1 \to p_2 \Box\models r}$$

(the rule for adding rules),

3.

$$\frac{\begin{array}{c} p_1 p_2 \Box\models p_1 p_2 \\ q_1\Box p_1 \to p_2 \Box q_2 \models p_1 r \end{array}}{q_1\Box p_1 \to p_2 \Box q_2 \models r p_2}$$

(the rule for normal transition).

Any word of the form described in the theorem is derivable in this calculus. To see that, consider the following example.

EXAMPLE 7 (continued)   Let us derive in $U^{\{|, T\}}$ the fact of the derivability of $\|$ in the calculus with designation (2.12). First derive a few facts concerning the derivability of axioms in some calculi without inference rules:

$$\Box\models, \quad |\Box\models|, \quad |T\Box\models|T, \quad |TT\Box\models|TT, \quad T\Box\models T, \quad T|\Box\models T|$$

(in this derivation we use, of course, only rules of group 1). Then by rule 2 we derive the fact of the derivability of the axiom of calculus (2.11) in (2.11):

$$\ldots, |\Box| \to TT\Box\models|, |\Box| \to TT\Box T \to |\Box\models|.$$

Finally, we conclude the derivation by modeling the transitions of our normal calculus (2.11):

$$\ldots NTT, NT|, N\|,$$

where N stands for the word (2.12). The initially given derivation in the calculus with designation N has the form

$|, TT, T|, \|$

and turns out to be precisely simulated by the last four words of the derivation we constructed. (The other seven words at the beginning of the derivation are in essence auxiliary, but all auxiliary words satisfy the theorem as well.)

The reader should already be familiar with induction on the length of derivation and can easily check that it is impossible to derive in U^A any words that are not supposed to be derivable.

The axiom clearly has the required form. It is easy to see that, whenever the premises of an inference rule of U^A have the required form, so does the conclusion. We check it for the most complicated rule only.

Let both premises of rule 3 be representable in the form NP. The first premise should also have the form $P_1 P_2 \Box \models P_1 P_2$, which is possible only if N is degenerate, that is, if $P = P_1 P_2$, $N = P_1 P_2 \Box \models$. Consequently, the values of p_1 and p_2 are necessarily words in A (at this point we realize, of course, that the sole purpose of introducing the first premise was to exclude unwanted substitutions for p_1 and p_2). The second ("real") premise of a normal transition also has the form NP for some N and P and should also be representable in the form specified in the rule, that is, in the form

$Q_1 \Box p_1 \rightarrow p_2 \Box Q_2 \models p_1 R.$

Then $p = p_1 R$, and N contains $p_1 \rightarrow p_2$ delimited by two squares. This means that the calculus designated by N contains the rule

$$\frac{P_1 p}{p P_2}.$$

By the induction hypothesis, there is a word P of the form $P_1 R$ derivable in this calculus. Consequently $R p_2$ is also derivable in it. If we look now at the conclusion of rule 3, we see that we have succeeded in deriving NRP_2. Hence the conclusion has the form required by the theorem. The calculus U^A has the desired properties.

Our joy that the constructed calculus is absolutely universal is somewhat marred by its dependence on the alphabet. When we are interested in some r.e. set, it makes no difference to us which letters are included in the alphabet of its representing calculus; so far as the alphabet of the set itself is concerned, it does not matter to us what its letters look like or even how many of them there are. Letters can be redenoted, coded in various ways; they are not essential. For this reason let me carry out a little standardization.

LEMMA (ON THE ONE-LETTER EXTENSION)   Every r.e. set in **A** can be represented by a normal calculus in the one-letter extension of **A**.

Proof   Let $(\mathbf{A}, K)$ be a representation of the set. Using Post's theorem, construct a normal calculus equivalent to K with respect to the alphabet of K (and consequently with respect to **A**). Let $\mathbf{A} = \{a_1, \ldots, a_k\}$, and let the alphabet of the normal calculus be

$$\{a_1, \ldots, a_k, a_{k+1}, \ldots, a_{k+l}\}.$$

Encode each word in this alphabet according to the following rules ($\xi \notin \mathbf{A}$; we denote the encoding of P by $k \lfloor P \rfloor$; Λ stands for the empty word):

$$k\lfloor a_i \rfloor = a_i \qquad (i = 1, \ldots, k),$$

$$k\lfloor a_{k+j} \rfloor = \xi a_1 \xi \qquad (j = 1, \ldots, l),$$

$$k\lfloor PQ \rfloor = k\lfloor P \rfloor K \lfloor Q \rfloor,$$

$$k\lfloor \Lambda \rfloor = \Lambda.$$

Consider the normal calculus whose axiom is the encoding of the old axiom and whose inference rules have the form

$$K\lfloor G \rfloor p \vdash pK\lfloor G' \rfloor,$$

where $Gp \vdash pG'$ is a rule of the old calculus. It is easy to see that this calculus has the required property.

Remark 6   The encoding of inference rules does not work for arbitrary canonical calculi. (Why?) Thus the lemma gives a solution of problem 4 from section 2.1, but it requires a preliminary transition to a normal calculus. This transition makes the derivations much longer, so that it is interesting to establish the possibility of a direct minimization of the auxiliary alphabet for arbitrary calculi (compare with remark 4). As a matter of fact, for every canonical calculus K over **A** one can construct an equivalent canonical calculus K' in the one-letter extension of **A** such that the length of a derivation in K' of any word in **A** is equal to the length of its derivation in K.

Let me introduce the following encoding of words in **A** by words in $\{0, 1\}$:

$$k\lfloor a_i \rfloor = 01^{\langle i \rangle}0 \qquad (i = 1, \ldots, k),$$

$$k\lfloor PQ \rfloor = k\lfloor P \rfloor k\lfloor Q \rfloor,$$

$$k\lfloor \Lambda \rfloor = \Lambda. \tag{2.14}$$

LEMMA (ON THE UNIVERSALITY OF THE TWO-LETTER ALPHABET)   For any alphabet **A**, a set of words in **A** is r.e. if and only if the set of codes of its elements is r.e.

The reader can easily prove this lemma (a similar proof is given for the lemma on the diagonal, which follows shortly).

Thus every r.e. set can essentially be described using only the alphabet $\{0, 1\}$. It follows that we can restrict our attention to normal calculi in $\{0, 1, 2\}$. Taking all this into account and using the calculus $U^{\{0,1,2\}}$, we can then say that the set U of words in $\{0, 1\}$ of the form $k[N]k[P]$, where N is a designation of a normal calculus in $\{0, 1, 2\}$ and P is a word derivable in that calculus, is r.e. At this point it is convenient to have in mind the following specialization of encoding (2.14):

$$k\lfloor 0 \rfloor = 010, \quad k\lfloor 1 \rfloor = 0110, \quad k\lfloor 2 \rfloor = 01110,$$

$$k\lfloor \rightarrow \rfloor = 01^{\langle 4 \rangle}0, \quad k\lfloor \square \rfloor = 01^{\langle 5 \rangle}0, \quad k\lfloor \models \rfloor = 01^{\langle 6 \rangle}0. \tag{2.15}$$

We call this set U *universal*. It is interesting to note that U can be represented by a calculus in $\{0, 1\}$; that is, it can be represented without auxiliary words, as in the case of $U^{\mathbf{A}}$.

The set U is r.e., but its complement $\bar{U}$ with respect to the set of all words in $\{0, 1\}$ is not. The method used in the proof of this fundamental fact goes back to the famous diagonal method of G. Kantor, the creator of set theory. The idea of this method can be explained as follows. Assume that we have a class K of sets, and for every set we define its "code" in some way. This code may sometimes be an element of its own set. Form the "diagonal set" D that consists of the codes of all those sets from K that do not include their own code. It turns out that $D \notin K$!

Digression on a Principled Barber

In the little Swiss canton of Kantorfeld there is a barber who shaves only those citizens of the canton who do not shave themselves. But for such citizens he makes no exceptions; he shaves all of them. Does the barber shave himself? If not, then there is a man whom he does not shave even though that man does not shave himself. If yes, then he shaves someone who shaves himself. How is this possible? Only in one case: If the barber is not a citizen of Kantorfeld!

Instead of "does not shave himself" let us say "does not contain its own code." Our "barber," the diagonal set, cannot possibly belong to K.

Here, for instance, is a proof of the fact that the set of all subsets of natural numbers is uncountable: Let $M_1, M_2, \ldots$ be a sequence of sets of natural numbers, and let the code of a set be its subscript in this sequence. Then the diagonal set does not belong to the sequence. Consequently, no enumeration of sets of natural numbers can possibly include all such sets.

Every uncountable set is, of course, not r.e., but we want to find a subset of the countable set of words in $\{0, 1\}$ that would not be r.e. Moreover, we want to find such a subset among the complements of r.e. sets. For these reasons the diagonal construction becomes somewhat more cumbersome.

Let K be the set of r.e. sets in $\{0, 1\}$ that is represented as the class of normal calculi in $\{0, 1, 2\}$. By the code of a set M I mean the word $k \lfloor N \rfloor$, which encodes the designation of the normal calculus representing M. (I assume that encoding (2.15) is used.) The diagonal set D consists of such $k \lfloor N \rfloor$ that $k \lfloor N \rfloor$ is not derivable in the calculus with the designation $k \lfloor N \rfloor$. Then $D \notin K$; that is, D is not r.e.

It remains to show how this leads to the conclusion that $\overline{U}$ is not r.e.

LEMMA (ON THE DIAGONAL)   Let M be an r.e. set of words in $\{0, 1\}$. Then the set M^∂ of words X such that $X k \lfloor X \rfloor \in M$ is also r.e.

Let M be represented by a calculus K, and let ξ_1, ξ_2 be letters not belonging to the alphabet of this calculus. Append ξ_1 on the left to each axiom and each line of each inference rule of K. Add to the calculus the axiom $\xi_2 \xi_2$ and the rules

$$\xi_2 p \xi_2 q \vdash \xi_2 p 0 \xi_2 q 010, \quad \xi_2 p \xi_2 q \vdash \xi_2 p 1 \xi_2 q 0110.$$

Finally, include the rule

$$\xi_1 pq, \quad \xi_2 p \xi_2 q \vdash p.$$

Obviously, the constructed calculus represents M^∂ (recall the proof of the recursive enumerability of the union of r.e. sets).

It is easy to see that the set of designations of normal calculi in $\{0, 1, 2\}$

is r.e. Then, by the lemma on page 26, the set M^K of the codes of these designations is also r.e..

Now consider the set

$$\bar{U}^{\partial} \cap M^K. \qquad\qquad\qquad (*)$$

A word belongs to this set if and only if it has the form $k\lfloor N\rfloor$, where the word

$$k\lfloor N\rfloor k\lfloor k\lfloor N\rfloor\rfloor \qquad\qquad\qquad (2.16)$$

belongs to $\bar{U}$. The latter condition means that $k\lfloor N\rfloor$ is not derivable in the calculus with the designation N (otherwise word (2.16) would be in U). Consequently, the set $(*)$ is the diagonal set D. This proves that $\bar{U}$ is not r.e.; if it were r.e., then $\bar{U}^{\partial}$ and D would also be r.e.

Let us call a set *decidable* if both the set and its complement are r.e. (If both M and its complement M^c are r.e., then we can organize the process of parallel generation of the elements of these sets. In this process each word will be generated at some point, and we will be able to determine whether it belongs to M or M^c. The use of the term "decidable" is connected with this possibility.) Thus U is an example of an undecidable r.e. set.

Problems

1.   Prove the lemma on the universality of the two-letter alphabet.

2.   Let us call a calculus S-*separated* if there are at least S letters between any two occurrences of variables in the premises of its inference rules. Transform an arbitrary calculus into an S-separated one so that the set of derivations does not change (that is, the new derivations have exactly the same structure as the old ones).

3.   Use problem 2 to prove the assertion from remark 6. Then change the proof in such a way that only 2-separatedness is used.

4.   Prove that U is strictly representable.

2.4   The Place Where You Stand: Local Calculi

It is easy to understand the great theoretical importance of Post's theorem and its potential applications to constructing various specializations of the apparatus of calculi. But the concept of a calculus itself looks perhaps somewhat unnatural.

As a matter of fact, what is the scheme of processing information by a normal calculus? The simplest elementary step is taking information from the beginning of the word that is being processed and moving the result of transforming this information to the end. One can imagine, of course, an administrator who receives the next paper, immediately processes it, and then stores it for a long time. It is possible to work in this way, but typical information processing systems work differently. In more adequate models of real-life systems, information is processed in one (finite!) field, which, however, can move (gradually!).

Here we immediately arrive at the concept of a *local* calculus, which is a canonical calculus with one axiom and with inference rules of the form

$$p_1 G p_2 \vdash p_1 G' p_2,$$

where p_1, p_2 are variables and G and G' are words in the alphabet of the calculus. For such rules we use the more compact notation

$$G \mapsto G'. \tag{2.17}$$

LOCALIZATION THEOREM   Every r.e. set can be represented by a local calculus (in an appropriate extension of the alphabet).

The theorem can be proved if for every normal calculus in **A** we construct a local calculus equivalent to it with respect to **A**. Consider a calculus

$$\{\mathbf{A}, \{p\}, \{R\}, \{G_1 p \vdash p G_1', \dots, G_N p \vdash p G_N'\}\}.$$

Extend **A** by adding the letters $\{b, e, \xi_0, \xi_1, \dots, \xi_N\}$, and construct the calculus with the axiom $\xi_0 R e$, the rules

$$b \xi_0 G_i \mapsto b \xi_i, \quad \xi_i x \mapsto x \xi_i (x \in A), \quad \xi_i e \mapsto \xi_0 G_i' e \ (i = 1, \dots, N),$$

which model the normal transition, the rules

$$x \xi_0 \mapsto \xi_0 x \qquad (x \in \mathbf{A}),$$

which allow ξ_0 to come back to the beginning of the word, and the rules

$$\xi_0 e \mapsto \xi_0, \quad b \xi_0 \mapsto,$$

which make it possible to eliminate all auxiliary letters. This local calculus has the required property. Prove it!

Notice that the letters of the alphabet

$$\{\xi_0, \xi_1, \ldots, \xi_N\} \tag{2.18}$$

play a special role in the calculus we have constructed; there is exactly one of these letters in each premise. All transformations in local transitions are done around the only occurrence of such a letter in the word. With this kind of organization of a local calculus, letters from alphabet (2.18) can naturally be called "shuttles," and the calculus itself is called a *shuttle calculus*. The possibility of processing any part of the word is due to the gradual motion of the shuttle along the word. Shuttle calculi completely realize the idea of a single field, of the local processing of information without the possibility of performing actions outside the field.

The calculus cannot be distracted, enticed by anything; the shuttle works where it is placed by its destiny!

Remark 7   We can narrow the field of work: Every r.e. set can be represented by a shuttle calculus in which all G and G' in inference rules contain at most two letters (that is, the shuttle knows itself and sees only one more letter). Another extension of the localization theorem is connected with the possibility of proving the lemma on the one-letter extension for local calculi.

2.5   The Calculus of Tallies

And, for low life, there were numbers,
Like cattle under the yoke,
Because all shades of meaning
Can be expressed by sensible numbers.
N. Gumilev

Recall the lemma on the universality of the two-letter alphabet. Once we start encoding words in one alphabet by words in another one, the meticulous reader could have asked at that time, "Why don't we use the one-letter alphabet?" As a matter of fact, every word can be encoded by a number, every number by a word. If we decide to encode words, let us do it to the end. And every number in base 1 notation is a word in the primitive one-letter alphabet, the alphabet of marks, or tallies. Thus all shades of meaning can be expressed using the one-letter alphabet alone. For instance, one can use this lemma:

LEMMA (ON THE UNIVERSALITY OF THE ONE-LETTER ALPHABET)   For any alphabet **A**, a set of words in **A** is r.e. if and only if the set of their codes is r.e., the codes being defined by

$$\text{if } \mathbf{A} = \{a_1, \ldots, a_k\}, \text{ then } k\lfloor Pa_i \rfloor = k\lfloor P \rfloor^{\langle k \rangle} 1^{\langle i \rangle} \tag{2.19}$$

($i = 1, \ldots, k$; it is assumed that $k\lfloor \Lambda \rfloor = \Lambda$).

The proof again follows the same pattern as in the lemma on the diagonal, only the rules containing ξ_2 look a little bit different:

$$\xi_1 p \xi_2 q \vdash \xi_2 p a_i \xi_2 q^{\langle k \rangle} 1^{\langle i \rangle} \qquad (i = 1, \ldots, k),$$

$$\xi_1 p, \quad \xi_2 p \xi_2 q \vdash q.$$

Thus, along with the "standard" introduced (r.e. sets in $\{0, 1\}$, normal calculi in $\{0, 1, 2\}$), we now have another standard: r.e. sets in $\{1\}$, normal calculi in $\{1, 2\}$ (the lemma on the one-letter extension is used here). The advantage of the new standard is that the same goals can be achieved by more restricted means. But there are disadvantages as well.

First, the encoding (2.14), even though it is not too economical, still makes the length of encoded words greater by at most a factor of $k + 2$. But for encoding (2.19),

$$k\lfloor a_k^{\langle n \rangle} \rfloor = 1^{\left\langle \frac{k^{n+1} - k}{k - 1} \right\rangle},$$

and no other encoding allows us to eliminate the exponential growth of the length of encoded words (see problem 1 on page 43). Obviously, such encodings are vitually inapplicable.

Second, encoding (2.14) allows a step-by-step simulation of the work of a calculus in **A**, under which the lengths of all derivations are preserved: Any derivation $p_1, \ldots, p_l$ in the given calculus becomes precisely the derivation $\lfloor p_1 \rfloor, \ldots, \lfloor p_l \rfloor$ in the new calculus (see problems 2–4 in section 2.3; the construction of the calculus of codes requires some attention and the use of S-separability). On the contrary, it turns out that in the case of the one-letter alphabet it is impossible to preserve the lengths of derivations.

Generally, processing words in the one-letter alphabet by means of canonical calculi is rather difficult. These problems are discussed in what follows; they are quite fundamental and useful for further applications.

The Calculus of Pairs

In this section I consider the problem of the possibility of constructing calculi over $\{1\}$ in which the role of auxiliary letters is reduced to a minimum.

THEOREM ON AUXILIARY PAIRS   Every r.e. set of words in $\{1\}$ can be represented by a calculus in $\{1, \square\}$ in which all derivable words contain at most one occurrence of $\square$.

To put it another way, the words derivable in the representing calculus are the elements of the given set plus some auxiliary words of the form $1^{\langle i \rangle} \square 1^{\langle j \rangle}$.

Proof   Let the given set be represented by the normal calculus

$$(\{1, 2\}, \{p\}, \{R\}, \{G_1 p \vdash pG_1', \ldots, G_N p \vdash pG_N'\}). \tag{2.20}$$

Introduce encoding (2.19), keeping in mind that $a_1 = 1, a_2 = 2$, and $k = 2$. We are going to construct an auxiliary calculus K in the alphabet

$$\{1, \xi_0, \xi_1, \ldots, \xi_N, \xi_{N+1}\}.$$

We take $k \lfloor R \rfloor \xi_0$ to be the axiom of K. K has the following four rules (q, r are variables of K):

$$qq1^{\langle i \rangle} \xi_0 r \vdash q\xi_0 r r 1^{\langle i \rangle}, \quad q\xi_0 r r 1^{\langle i \rangle} \vdash qq1^{\langle i \rangle} \xi_0 r \quad (i = 1, 2).$$

These rules make it possible, for any two words P_1 and P_2 in the alphabet $\{1, 2\}$ to transform $k \lfloor P_1 P_2 \rfloor \xi_0$ into $k \lfloor P_1 \rfloor \xi_0 k \lfloor P_2^T \rfloor$ and back. (Here P_2^T stands for the "reversed" P_2, that is, the result of reading P_2 "backward.") For each rule of the given normal calculus, we add this group of four rules to K ($j = 1, \ldots, N$):

$$\frac{k \lfloor G_j \rfloor \xi_0 r}{\xi_j r}, \quad \frac{q\xi_j r r 1^{\langle i \rangle}}{qq1^{\langle i \rangle} \xi_j r} \quad (i = 1, 2), \quad \frac{q\xi_j}{q\xi_0 k \lfloor G_j'^T \rfloor},$$

which obviously models the given rule. Finally, add the rules

$$\frac{q\xi_0}{q\xi_{N+1}}, \quad \frac{qq1\xi_{N+1} r}{q\xi_{N+1} r 1}, \quad \frac{\xi_{N+1} r}{r},$$

which do the decoding, that is, which transform words of the form $k \lfloor 1^{\langle n \rangle} \rfloor \xi_0$ into $1^{\langle n \rangle}$.

It is easy to show by induction on the length of the derivation that K is equivalent to the calculus (2.20) with respect to $\{1\}$ and that every word derivable in K contains at most one occurrence of an auxiliary letter.

Now let us transform K as follows. We translate every word of the form

$$Q\xi_j R \qquad (j = 0, 1, \dots, N + 1), \tag{2.21}$$

where Q, R are words in the alphabet $\{1, q, r\}$, by $Q \square R^{\langle N+2 \rangle} 1^{\langle j \rangle}$. Replace each line of each inference rule of K as well as its axiom by its translation, which is a word in $\{1, 0, q, r\}$. (The only line that does not have the form (2.21) is the conclusion r of the last rule of inference; we leave that line as it is.) The reader will not find it difficult to check that the calculus constructed in this way has the required property.

We have adapted the machinery of canonical calculi to work with pairs of numbers. With some more work, we can model this adaptation without using delimiters. The idea of this modeling becomes clear from example 8.

EXAMPLE 8   Denote the word $1^{\langle 2^{\mu} \cdot 3^{\nu} \rangle}$ by $f(1^{\langle \mu \rangle} \square 1^{\langle \nu \rangle})$. Consider a rule of a canonical calculus in $\{1, \square\}$ of the form

$$\frac{q^{\langle \alpha \rangle} 1^{\langle \beta \rangle} \square r^{\langle \gamma \rangle} 1^{\langle \delta \rangle}}{q^{\langle \alpha' \rangle} 1^{\langle \beta' \rangle} \square r^{\langle \gamma' \rangle} 1^{\langle \delta' \rangle}}.$$

The transition by this rule is modeled by the following group of rules:

$$\frac{\xi_0 p^{\langle 2^{\beta} \cdot 3^{\delta} \rangle}}{\xi_1 p} \qquad \text{(checking that the premise has the form } f(1^{\langle x+\beta \rangle} \square 1^{\langle y+\delta \rangle}))$$

$$\frac{\xi_1 p^{\langle 2^{\alpha} \rangle}}{\xi_1 p^{\langle 5 \rangle}} \qquad \text{(checking step by step that } x = \alpha x'; \; x' \text{ is coded by the powers}$$

of 5)

$$\xi_1 pp1 \vdash \xi_2 pp1$$

$$\frac{\xi_2 p^{\langle 3^{\gamma} \rangle}}{\xi_2 p^7} \qquad \text{(checking similarly that } y = \gamma y' \text{ and coding } y' \text{ by the powers}$$

of 7)

$$\xi_2 p^{\langle 3 \rangle} 1^{\langle i \rangle} \vdash \xi_3 p^{\langle 3 \rangle} 1^{\langle i \rangle} \quad (i = 1, 2)$$

$$\frac{\xi_3 p^{\langle 5 \rangle}}{\xi_3 p^{2\alpha'}}, \quad \frac{\xi_3 p^{\langle 5 \rangle} 1^{\langle i \rangle}}{\xi_4 p^5 1^{\langle i \rangle}} \qquad \text{(decoding the 5's; } i = 1, \dots, 4)$$

$$\frac{\xi_4 p^{\langle 7 \rangle}}{\xi_4 p^{3\gamma'}}, \quad \frac{\xi_4 p^{\langle 7 \rangle} 1^{\langle i \rangle}}{\xi_5 p^7 1^{\langle i \rangle}} \qquad \text{(decoding the 7's; } i = 1, \dots, 6)$$

$$\xi_5 p \vdash \xi_0 p^{\langle 2^{\beta'} \cdot 3^{\delta'} \rangle} \quad \text{(modeling is completed)}.$$

The result of the work of this group of rules is the transition from

$$\xi_0 f(1^{\langle \alpha x' + \beta \rangle} \Box 1^{\langle \gamma y' + \delta \rangle})$$

to

$$\xi_0 f(1^{\langle \alpha' x' + \beta' \rangle} \Box 1^{\langle \gamma' y' + \delta' \rangle}).$$

We say that a calculus *quasi-represents* a set M of numbers if a word of the form $1^{\langle 2^n \rangle}$ is derivable in it if and only if $1^{\langle n \rangle} \in M$. (Notice that this definition allows us to use words in $\{1\}$ as auxiliary, so long as they do not have the form $1^{\langle 2^n \rangle}$.) By applying the idea of example 8 to the calculus constructed in the last theorem, we arrive at the calculus that quasi-represents the given r.e. set of numbers and such that all auxiliary words begin with an auxiliary letter and have no other occurrences of auxiliary letters. This construction leads to two theorems: one for restricted calculi and one for calculi with labels.

Restricted Calculi.   The method used at the end of the proof of the last theorem for reducing the number of auxiliary letters, skillfully applied to the last calculus, gives the following corollary:

THEOREM   Every r.e. set of numbers can be quasi-represented by a restricted calculus, that is, by a calculus that has the null word as the only axiom and whose rules have the form

$$p^{\langle \alpha \rangle} 1^{\langle \beta \rangle} \vdash p^{\langle \alpha' \rangle} 1^{\langle \beta' \rangle}.$$

Calculi with Labels.   At the price of allowing two-premise rules, we can get rid of the prefix "quasi" while retaining the other properties of the machinery that are of interest to us. Consider the calculus

$$\left\{ \{1, \xi_0, \xi_1\}, \{p, q\}, \{\xi_0 1, \xi_1 1\}, \left\{ \frac{\xi_0 p}{\xi_0 pp}, \frac{\xi_1 pqq}{\xi_1 pqpqq 1} \right\} \right\}.$$

All words derivable in this calculus have one of two forms:

$$\xi_0 1^{\langle 2^n \rangle}, \quad \xi_1 1^{\langle 2^n + n \rangle} \qquad (n = 0, 1, \dots).$$

In the proof of this assertion we have to use the fact that a word of the form $1^{\langle 2^n + n \rangle}$ can be written in the form PQQ, where PQ is a power of 2, in exactly one way. By using this calculus to "take the logarithm base 2," as has been done many times (see the lemmas on the universality of alphabets and the lemma on the diagonal), we can prove the following corollary:

COROLLARY   Every r.e. set of numbers can be represented by a calculus in $\{1, \xi\}$ whose auxiliary words all have the form $\xi 1^{\langle n \rangle}$.

For alphabets containing more than one letter, this can be proved even more easily. Thus we have the following theorem:

THEOREM ON THE UNIQUE LABEL   For any alphabet $\mathbf{A}$ and an r.e. set M of words in $\mathbf{A}$, one can construct a representing calculus in which, besides the elements of M, only words of the form ξP are derivable, where P is a word in $\mathbf{A}$ and ξ is a fixed letter not in $\mathbf{A}$.

In example 8, we encoded tuples of numbers by the powers of primes. But this idea can also be reversed, and a number can be encoded by the tuple of exponents in its decompositions into a product of primes. Obviously, this is much more economical.

EXAMPLE 8 (continued)   Encode a word of the form

$$\xi_i 1^{\langle 2^\mu \cdot 3^\nu \cdot 5^\omega \cdot 7^\rho \rangle} \qquad (i = 0, 1, \ldots, 5)$$

by the word $1^{\langle i \rangle} \square 1^{\langle \mu \rangle} \square 1^{\langle \nu \rangle} \square 1^{\langle \omega \rangle} \square 1^{\langle \rho \rangle}$. Replace the group of rules constructed in the example by the following group:

$$\square 1^{\langle \beta \rangle} p_1 \square 1^{\langle \delta \rangle} p_2 \square p_3 \square p_4 \vdash 1 \square p_1 \square p_2 \square p_3 \square p_4,$$

$$1 \square 1^{\langle \alpha \rangle} p_1 \square p_2 \square p_3 \square p_4 \vdash 1 \square p_1 \square p_2 \square 1 p_3 \square p_4,$$

$$1 \square \square p_2 \square p_3 \square p_4 \vdash 11 \square \square p_2 \square p_3 \square p_4,$$

$$11 \square p_1 \square 1^{\langle \gamma \rangle} p_2 \square p_3 \square p_4 \vdash 11 \square p_1 \square p_2 \square p_3 \square 1 p_4,$$

$$11 \square p_1 \square \square p_3 \square p_4 \vdash 111 \square p_1 \square \square p_3 \square p_4, \ldots.$$

The comparison between the operation of this group and the initially given rule (2.22) shows that we lost in terms of the number of separators but that we gained in the simplicity of each rule. This is similar to Post's second reduction but has a number of technical advantages.

This leads us to the following concept. A *k-local calculus* is a canonical calculus in $\{1, \square\}$ whose only axiom has exactly k occurrences of $\square$ and whose rules have the form

$$\frac{1^{\langle l_0 \rangle} p_0 \square 1^{\langle l_1 \rangle} p_1 \square 1^{\langle l_2 \rangle} p_2 \square \ldots \square 1^{\langle l_k \rangle} p_k}{1^{\langle l_0' \rangle} p_0 \square 1^{\langle l_1' \rangle} p_1 \square 1^{\langle l_2' \rangle} p_2 \square \ldots \square 1^{\langle l_k' \rangle} p_k}.$$

Some of the p_i may be missing; that is, some p_i denote here the null word both in the premise and in the conclusion. Every word provable in a k-local calculus has exactly k occurrences of $\square$; that is, every word encodes a vector of $k + 1$ natural numbers. We have already encountered such calculi (see example 4 in chapter 1 and example 7 in this chapter).

Notice that each transition of a k-local calculus consists in changing k fixed places in the word being transformed, changing the neighborhoods of the squares.

THEOREM ON k-LOCALIZATION   For every r.e. set of numbers, one can construct a 3-local calculus in which a word of the form $\square 1^{\langle n \rangle} \square \square$ is derivable if and only if $1^{\langle n \rangle} \in M$.

The detailed proof of this theorem is based on the calculus of pairs and on the ideas of example 8; the difficulties are only technical. To make k as small as possible, we "copy" the "contents" of p_3 (that is, the information between the second and the third squares) to p_1 before the word with p_2 starts. Then p_3 can be reused and p_4 becomes redundant. (In terms of restricted calculi, we can use just the powers of 2, 3, and 5, not powers of 7.) In this way we can achieve $k = 3$.

The universality of the apparatus of 3-local calculi is demonstrated in another way in chapter 3. In this book we use the universality of local, k-local, and restricted calculi many times.

Problems

1. For every encoding of words in an m-letter alphabet by words in a one-letter alphabet that assigns different codes to different words, prove that the maximum of the lengths of $k \lfloor P \rfloor$ over all words P of length n grows as m^n.

2. Let K^k be a calculus representing the set of codes of the words derivable in K. We are interested in comparing the lengths of derivations of a word P in K and the lengths of derivations of $k \lfloor P \rfloor$ in K^k. Prove the possibility of preserving the lengths of derivations for encoding into the two-letter alphabet, and construct K for which the lengths must inevitably grow for encoding into the one-letter alphabet.

3. Give a detailed proof of the theorem on auxiliary pairs.

4. Prove the theorem on restricted calculi.

5. Prove the theorem on the unique label.

6. Prove the theorem on k-localization.

3 Deductive Systems and Algorithms

There are many ties between the concept of a deductive system and the concept of an algorithm. Being a special case of calculi, algorithms can serve not only as a language for their specification but also as a language in which some essential properties of calculi can be stated in a natural way (recall, for instance, the two descriptions of decidable sets in chapter 2). Ties of this sort are the subject of this chapter.

3.1 What Is an Algorithm?

Resolved: that two "Minsk" machines be purchased, and one Minsky machine.
A Russian joke about administrators

The development of the precise concept of an algorithm was a mathematical achievement of the twentieth century. Familiarity with some fundamental aspects of the theory of algorithms is essential for work in many different areas, especially in the areas connected with the use of computers. There are many books about algorithms. I recommend [16] as a first introduction, [12] for a deeper study; see also [17]. Here I cover only the topics needed for the understanding of the rest of the book.

The Idealized Computer

In this section I discuss one possible precise definition of an algorithm that is sufficiently simple and at the same time close to real computers. (Various equivalent definitions were proposed in the 1930s and 1940s by A. Turing, Post, A. Markov, and others).

Imagine the following "computer" M. M has a finite number of "cells," each cell capable of storing an arbitrary integer. M can perform the following operations (*arithmetical instructions*) with the numbers in the cells:

1. $+\alpha\beta\gamma$ (add the numbers in the cells α and β and place the result in γ),
2. $-\alpha\beta\gamma$ (subtract the number in β from the number in α and place the result in γ),
3. $\times\alpha\beta\gamma$ (multiply the numbers in α and β and place the result in γ),
4. $:\alpha\beta\gamma$ (divide the number in β into the number in α and place the incomplete quotient in γ; we set $x:0 = 1$).

The operation of the machine is defined by a *program*, that is, a list of numbered instructions, which may contain, in addition to the arithmetical instructions listed, the *control instructions*

5. $\to n$ (jump to instruction number n),

6. $\to(\alpha)n$ (if the number in α is positive, then branch to instruction number n),

7. HALT (terminate execution).

In all cases except those mentioned in instructions 5–7, the computer, having executed an instruction, proceeds to the instruction next to it in the program. The *input* of M in the process of execution of a program Π is the contents of all cells before the execution of the first instruction; the *output* is the contents of all cells after termination.

If we want to describe a program Π that computes the values of a function $f(x_1,\ldots,x_n)$, where f is an integer-valued function of integer variables, then we should additionally specify n input cells and one output cell (not necessarily different from the input cells). If the contents of the input cells at the beginning of execution are $x_1,\ldots,x_n$ and if all other cells contain 0, then the output cell must contain after termination the value $f(x_1,\ldots,x_n)$, and the contents of the other cells do not matter.

EXAMPLE 9 We want to implement Euclid's algorithm for computing the greatest common divisor on M. We need three cells: 1, 2, and 3; they initially contain a, b, and 0, respectively. We assume that a and b are positive. The first column in the table that follows is the program, and the other columns show the operation of the program for the input 6, 8, 0:

Program		Contents of the cells			
1.	-123	6, 8, -2	6, 2, 4	4, 2, 2	2, 2, 0
2.	$\to(3)6$				
3.	-213	6, 8, 2			2, 2, 0
4.	$\to(3)8$				
5.	HALT				HALT
6.	-121		4, 2, 4	2, 2, 2	
7.	$\to1$				
8.	-212	6, 2, 2			
9.	$\to1$				

This concept has much in common with the organization of any computer, even though real computers have much larger possibilities in almost all respects. In particular, they have many more instructions (arithmetical operations with floating-point numbers, logical operations, etc.) and are able to modify the program in the process of computation. But real computers are finite objects, whereas our idealization permits processing a potentially infinite amount of information. Without loss of generality we can restrict the number of cells in the definition and even the size of the program so long as the cells are allowed to contain arbitrarily large numbers. It is this assumption that makes idealized machines fundamentally different from real computers. (The solution of practical problems is usually not affected by this difference because the memory of a modern computer is sufficiently large.)

But, having allowed the potentially infinite capacity of a cell, we can assert that *any computational process that has ever been or will be invented can be implemented (in principle) on a machine of the described type.* This assertion is known as the *Turing thesis* (Turing himself proposed it for another but equivalent version of a precise definition of an algorithm). The thesis cannot be proved mathematically; however, there are serious reasons to accept it.

The concept of a *Minsky machine* is a special case of the described class of machines. It is even simpler and more convenient for further applications. Select a fixed cell that always has the number 1 in it (denote it by **1**); in addition, the machine will have exactly two cells, which are called *working cells*. The only arithmetical instructions are $+\alpha 1\alpha$ and $-\alpha 1\alpha$, where α is a working cell. The instruction $-\alpha 1\alpha$ can be executed only if α does not contain 0. If the input does not contain negative numbers, then this condition guarantees that no negative numbers will emerge as results.

EXAMPLE 10   Let us compute the incomplete quotient and the remainder obtained from dividing x by 3; before the computation begins, x is written in cell 1 (and 0 in cell 2); after termination, cell 1 will contain the remainder, and cell 2 the quotient. The program and an example of its execution (for $x = 8$) are as follows:

Program	Contents of the cells		
1. −111	7, 0	4, 1	1, 2
2. →15			
3. +111			2, 2
4. HALT			HALT
5. −111	6, 0	3, 1	0, 2
6. →19			
7. +111			
8. →3			1, 2
9. −111	5, 0	2, 1	
10. 212	5, 1	2, 2	
11. →1			

It is possible to model any computation on a Minsky machine. More precisely, let $f(x)$ be an algorithmically computable function (we can assume that this is a natural-valued function of a natural argument that can be computed on an idealized machine). Then we have the following:

MINSKY'S THEOREM   One can construct a Minsky machine that, given a pair $(2^x, 0)$ as input, terminates if and only if the process of computation of $f(x)$ terminates, and returns the output $2^{f(x)}$ in cell 1.

So a computation of any degree of difficulty can be performed using the ability to add and subtract 1 and recognize 0! (See problem 9.)

Problems

1. For the idealized computer, write programs to compute the values of the following functions:
(a) $y = (x^2 + 1)(x^3 - 1)$,
(b) $y = \max\{x_1^2 + x_2^2, x_3^2\}$,
(c) $y = x_1^{x_2}$.

2. Write a program to compute the roots of a quadratic equation.

3. Write a program to check whether x is a multiple of y.

4. Write a program to check whether a given number is prime.

5. If we change the condition that $0:0 = 1$ and decide, for instance, that the machine stops when a division by zero is attempted, then some computations of values of computable functions will become impossible. Why? How should the system of concepts be modified so that the machine will stop in case of division by zero and yet still be able to compute every computable function?

6. Using a Minsky machine, check whether a given number has the form $3^n + 2$.

7. Construct a Minsky machine to transform any number of the form 3^n into 2^{n+2}.

8. Using the ideas of section 2.5 of chapter 2, prove Minsky's theorem.

9. Define a machine completely similar to the Minsky machine but with three working cells. Show how to compute on this machine any unary algorithmically computable function without the 2^n-encoding.

3.2 Algorithmic Undecidability

Assume that we are interested in a certain class of problems. Without loss
of generality, assume that information about the data given in each problem
and about the solution is encoded by numbers (see section 2.5 of chapter
2). A machine is said to *solve* this class of problems if for each particular
problem in this class it terminates for the code of the data of this problem
and produces the code of its solution. The precise concept of an algorithm
makes it possible to state precisely the question of whether a class of
problems is decidable or undecidable.

In particular, it becomes possible to prove for some classes of problems
that they *cannot be solved by any machine*.

Algorithmically undecidable classes of problems have been found in
various branches of mathematics, including the theory of algorithms itself.
For instance, let Π be a Minsky machine program and x a natural number.
The problem $P_{\Pi,x}$ calls for deciding whether the Minsky machine with the
program Π and the initial state $x, 0$ terminates or proceeds for an infinitely
long time. It is possible to construct a machine Π_0 so that the class of
problems $P_{\Pi_0,x}$ (with arbitrary x) is undecidable. In this case we say that
the *termination problem for Π_0 is undecidable*. This result can be used to
construct a deductive system with the *undecidable derivability problem*, that
is, to construct a calculus such that it is impossible, given a word (in the
alphabet of the calculus), to decide algorithmically whether the word is
derivable. Let us construct such a calculus.

Let Π be a Minsky machine program with the undecidable termination
problem, and let N be the number of its instructions. We construct a 2-local
calculus whose derivable objects have the form $1^{\langle l \rangle}\square 1^{\langle x \rangle}\square 1^{\langle y \rangle}$, where
$1 \leqslant l \leqslant N, x \geqslant 0, y \geqslant 0$. There are one or two rules of the calculus corresponding to each instruction of Π, as follows:

1. The rule corresponding to the instruction $l: +111$ is

$$\frac{1^{\langle l \rangle}\square p_1 \square p_2}{1^{\langle l+1 \rangle}\square 1 p_1 \square p_2}.$$

2. The rule corresponding to the instruction $l: +212$ is

$$\frac{1^{\langle l \rangle}\square p_1 \square p_2}{1^{\langle l+1 \rangle}\square p_1 \square 1 p_2}.$$

3. The rule corresponding to the instruction $l: \to n$ is

$$\frac{1^{\langle l \rangle} \square p_1 \square 1 p_2}{1^{\langle n \rangle} \square p_1 \square p_2}.$$

4. The two rules corresponding to the instruction $l: -111$ are

$$\frac{1^{\langle l \rangle} \square \square p_2}{1^{\langle L \rangle} \square \square p_2} \quad \text{and} \quad \frac{1^{\langle l \rangle} \square 1 p_1 \square p_2}{1^{\langle l+1 \rangle} \square p_1 \square p_2}.$$

5. The two rules corresponding to the instruction $l: -212$ are

$$\frac{1^{\langle l \rangle} \square p_1 \square}{1^{\langle L \rangle} \square p_1 \square} \quad \text{and} \quad \frac{1^{\langle l \rangle} \square p_1 \square 1 p_2}{1^{\langle l+1 \rangle} \square p_1 \square p_2}.$$

6. The rules corresponding to the instruction $l: \to(1)n$ are

$$\frac{1^{\langle l \rangle} \square 1 p_1 \square p_2}{1^{\langle n \rangle} \square 1 p_1 \square p_2} \quad \text{and} \quad \frac{1^{\langle l \rangle} \square \square p_2}{1^{\langle l+1 \rangle} \square \square p_2},$$

and the rules corresponding to the instruction $l: \to(2)n$ are

$$\frac{1^{\langle l \rangle} \square p_1 \square 1 p_2}{1^{\langle n \rangle} \square p_1 \square 1 p_2} \quad \text{and} \quad \frac{1^{\langle l \rangle} \square p_1 \square}{1^{\langle l+1 \rangle} \square p_1 \square}.$$

7. The rules corresponding to the instruction $L: \text{HALT}$ are

$$\frac{1^{\langle L \rangle} \square 1 p_1 \square p_2}{1^{\langle L \rangle} \square p_1 \square p_2} \quad \text{and} \quad \frac{1^{\langle L \rangle} \square p_1 \square 1 p_2}{1^{\langle L \rangle} \square p_1 \square p_2}.$$

(Here we assume that all the l's are distinct and that L is the fixed number of a HALT instruction; the uniqueness of HALT does not restrict generality.) The only axiom is $1 \square 1^{\langle x \rangle} \square$. It is easy to see that the process of derivation in this calculus is uniquely determined and precisely models the work of the machine with the initial state x, 0. In the last stage of computation, if the machine stops, then the process of derivation can still be continued by rules 7 until the word $|^{\langle L \rangle} \square \square$ is obtained. We see that this word is derivable in the calculus under consideration if and only if Π terminates for the initial state x, 0. The undecidability of the class of problems $P_{\Pi, x}$ also means that the following problem is undecidable: Given an axiom $|\square|^{\langle x \rangle} \square$, determine whether $|^{\langle L \rangle} \square \square$ can be derived.

Let us now "invert" the calculus we have constructed. Make $|^{\langle L \rangle} \square \square$ the axiom, and interchange the premise and the conclusion in each inference rule. We call the new calculus the *inverse* of the initial one. In this calculus a word of the form $|\square|^{\langle x \rangle}\square$ is derivable if and only if the answer to the problem $P_{\Pi,x}$ is yes. This shows that the derivability problem for the inverse calculus is undecidable. Such calculi are called *undecidable*. Thus we have proved the following theorem:

THEOREM ON UNDECIDABILITY   There exists an undecidable 2-local calculus.

It is easy to see that we are dealing here with a fact already known to us in a somewhat different form. First, a calculus is undecidable if and only if the set of words derivable in it is undecidable. So the theorem asserts the existence of an r.e. set whose complement is not r.e. (see chapter 2). Second, the previous chapter contains a direct proof of the existence of an undecidable k-local calculus for $k = 3$ (see the theorem on k-localization). Making k smaller in the theorem is connected with the use of the encoding based on the function 2^x in the Minsky machine, that is, with the use of a quasi-representation of a set (see chapter 2). The use of a quasi-representation would also have allowed us to make k smaller in the theorem on k-localization; then we would have obtained a direct proof of the undecidability of 2-local calculi not based on Minsky's theorem, given here without proof.

The Universality Criterion

Oh, how to descry the vague face of Nature?
Wherever I look, there are vaults, vaults, vaults.
V. Kushner

When modeling real-life processes by calculi, we encounter the problem of selecting the class of calculi appropriate for describing the processes we are interested in. For a more narrow class, the difference between the model and the process is greater, and the reduction is more rough. But, if reductions to classes of simpler calculi are not used, then the investigation is not interesting. The wider the class is, the more difficult it is to express in its terms something specific about the modeled processes. Thus reductions are necessary, but they should be such that the specific features of the model still reflect the specific features of the processes. To this end, the possibility of modeling arbitrarily complex processes should be retained.

In many cases, it is convenient to understand this requirement as the possibility of representing an arbitrary r.e. set in the framework of the class under consideration. This is the *universality criterion*. It looks strangely "intramathematical"; it does not seem to have anything to do with "natural science." But there are several reasons for this choice. In particular, once we agree to model something by calculi, we are not going to go outside the limits of recursive enumerability. The class of arbitrary calculi satisfies the criterion; hence nothing that can be of use to us is lost. But, perhaps, the criterion is too liberal and allows classes of calculi that are too wide. Well, this is possible, but the many reductions we have done show that arbitrarily complex undecidable sets can be generated using limited deductive means. Such deductive means always express explicitly only the simplest possibilities of the modeled processes, but this will not prevent us from conducting the qualitative analysis of the situation in probabilistic terms and drawing qualitative conclusions. Mainly, we are going to study problems related to the concept of freedom of choice in the system.

4 Probabilistic Calculi and Deductive Information

I have proclaimed and illustrated the fact that the theory of deductive systems is a natural apparatus for modeling nondeterministic processes. In many cases, of course, concepts of the theory of probability have to be used in these models too; in particular, probability measures have to be introduced on sets of derivations. The use of probabilistic ideas turns out to be useful both for valid modeling of the processes under study and, more unexpectedly, for the investigation of the calculi themselves and for comparing them to each other.

I can give here only a brief summary of the necessary facts about probabilities and information. The reader can find more details, for instance, in [18] and [19].

4.1 Probable and Improbable Derivations

We hate and love by chance.
A conjecture

With the exception of the special case of deterministic calculi, deductive systems define a set of potentially derivable objects, without predetermining how exactly a particular derivation will develope and, consequently, which objects will actually be derived. Once the functioning of the system is started, some of its states may become inaccessible, some trajectories may become more plausible than others, etc. It becomes possible to talk about the probability of this or that continuation of a given derivation, which, in its turn, makes it possible to define the probability of deriving a given word. We arrive at the notion of a *probabilistic calculus.*

Determining the actual probabilities of continuations of derivations may be difficult or even outright impossible (if it is difficult to reproduce the work of the system). But even in this case the concept of a probabilistic calculus turns out to be useful and may help to clarify the qualitative picture of the processes under consideration (see part II).

The investigation of this concept leads to a number of problems, which are discussed here for the simplest case (see [20]).

Let K be a canonical calculus of the form $\{\mathbf{A}, \mathbf{P}, \{R_0\}, \{\Pi_1, \ldots, \Pi_m\}\}$, where $\Pi_1, \ldots, \Pi_m$ are one-premise rules such that the result of applying any of them to any word derivable in K is uniquely defined. This condition is satisfied, for example, for shuttle calculi (see chapter 2) and for normal calculi. (For normal calculi the uniqueness of application holds for all words; for shuttle calculi it is satisfied only for derivable words or, more precisely, for the words containing one occurrence of the shuttle.)

An *analyzed derivation* in K is any list ξ of the form

$$R_0, R_1 \langle k_1, s_1 \rangle, R_2 \langle k_2, s_2 \rangle, \ldots, R_l \langle k_l, s_l \rangle, \qquad (4.1)$$

where $l \geqslant 0$, $R_0, R_1, \ldots, R_l$ are words in $\mathbf{A}$, $0 \leqslant k_1 \leqslant 0$, $0 \leqslant k_2 \leqslant 1, \ldots,$ $0 \leqslant k_l \leqslant l - 1$, $1 \leqslant s_1 \leqslant m, \ldots, 1 \leqslant s_l \leqslant m$, and for all i $(1 \leqslant i \leqslant l)$

$$R_{k_i} \vdash_{\Pi_{s_i}} R_i.$$

The last condition means that R_i is derivable from R_{k_i} by one application of Π_{s_i}. The list $R_0, R_1, \ldots, R_l$ is called the *derivation associated with* ξ; by $d(\xi)$ we denote its length, that is, $l + 1$.

A *probabilistic calculus* is a pair $\langle K, \mathscr{P} \rangle$, where $\mathscr{P}$ is an algorithm applicable to any analyzed derivation that assigns to every ξ of the form (4.1) a matrix

$$\{r_{ks}(\xi)\} \qquad (r_{ks}(\xi) \geqslant 0; k = 0, \ldots, l; s = 1, \ldots, m)$$

for which $\sum_{k,s} r_{ks}(\xi) = 1$. Here r_{ks} is interpreted as the probability of continuing ξ by applying Π_s to R_k. This allows us to define inductively the *probability of an analyzed derivation*:

1. If $\xi = R_0$, then $p[\xi] = 1$.
2. If $\xi = \eta, R \langle k, s \rangle$, then $p[\xi] = p[\eta] \cdot r_{ks}(\eta)$.

Now we can calculate the *probability of a derivation B*. To this end, denote by M_B the set of analyzed derivations with the associated derivation B. Then

$$p[B] = \sum_{\xi \in M_B} p[\xi].$$

It is also clear now how to compute the probability of a given word: Take the sum of the probabilities of all derivations that end in the given word and that have no other occurrences of that word.

EXAMPLE 11   Consider the calculus

$$\{\{|\}, \{q\}, \{|\}, \{q \vdash qq, q \vdash q|\}\},$$

and introduce a probability measure by means of the algorithm $\mathscr{A}$ transforming any derivation of the form (4.1) into the $2 \times (l + 1)$ matrix

$$\begin{pmatrix} 0 & \cdots & 0 & p_1 \\ 0 & \cdots & 0 & p_2 \end{pmatrix} \quad (p_1 + p_2 = 1).$$

In this probabilistic calculus a derivation can be continued only by applying one of the inference rules to the last word of the derivation. Let us compute the probability of the following derivation B:

|, ||, |||, ||||.

B is the associated derivation for the following four analyzed derivations:

|, ||⟨0, 1⟩, |||⟨1, 2⟩, ||||⟨2, 2⟩,

|, ||⟨0, 2⟩, |||⟨1, 2⟩, ||||⟨2, 2⟩,

|, ||⟨0, 1⟩, |||⟨1, 2⟩, ||||⟨1, 1⟩,

|, ||⟨0, 2⟩, |||⟨1, 2⟩, ||||⟨1, 1⟩.

The probability of each of the last two derivations is 0, because they contain applications of an inference rule to a word other than the last. The probabilities of the first two analyzed derivations are $p_1 p_2 p_2$ and $p_2 p_2 p_2$. Thus the total probability $p[B]$ is p_2^2. If we want to know the probability of deriving the word |||| in our calculus then we should add to this number the probability of the derivation |, ||, |||| (which can easily be computed and equals p_1).

The actual computation of the probability of deriving a given word can be difficult because of the possibility of infinitely many derivations of the same word. Even in our simple example, if applying inference rules to arbitrary words were allowed, then even for the word ||| it would have been necessary to take into account all derivations of the form

|, ||, $R_1, R_2, \ldots, R_N$, |||,

where all R_i are different from |||.

With the introduction of probabilistic calculi, the modeling possibilities of our apparatus become almost unlimited. In particular, it becomes possible to replace rigid schemes of the algorithmic enumeration of sets by "soft," "fuzzy" descriptions using such phrases as "derivable with a sufficiently high probability." The hypothesis that such quasi-probabilistic concepts reflect the essence of human intellect better than deterministic algorithms of information processing is quite fashionable now. There are many arguments in favor of this view.

This hypothesis would be especially convincing if probabilistic calculi led us outside of the class of r.e. sets; however, this is impossible. For any probabilistic calculus and any real δ, the set of words that is derivable with a probability greater than δ is r.e.

Thus probabilities do not help us extend the class of describable sets. It is known, however, that algorithms based on the probabilistic approach are in many cases more efficient; in other words, one may get with the help of probabilistic calculi more feasible descriptions of r.e. sets. In connection with that it is important to know under what conditions the probabilistic organization of a derivation is consistent with the probability of the derivability of each derivable word being 1.

We say that an algorithm $\mathscr{P}$ *prohibits derivation cutoff* if for all ξ, k, and s the inapplicability of Π_s to R_k implies $r_{ks}(\xi) = 0$ (that is, if $\mathscr{P}$ cannot select the pair R_k, Π_s for application). We say that $\mathscr{P}$ is a *complete algorithm* if $r_{ks}(\xi) = 0$ only in the following three cases:

1. Π_s is not applicable to R_k;
2. ξ contains an occurrence of a word $R_{k'}$ such that $R_k \vdash_{\Pi_s} R_{k'}$;
3. ξ contains an occurrence of a word $R_{k'}$ such that $R_k = R_{k'}$ and $r_{k's}(\xi) \neq 0$.

$\mathscr{P}$ is *equiprobabilistic* if for every ξ all nonzero elements of the matrix $\{r_{ks}(\xi)\}$ are equal to each other.

The reader can easily prove that for a complete $\mathscr{P}$ every word derivable in K is derivable with some nonzero probability in the probabilistic calculus $\langle K, \mathscr{P} \rangle$. It is somewhat more difficult to prove that, for a complete equiprobabilistic algorithm that prohibits derivation cutoff, every derivable word is derivable in $\langle K, \mathscr{P} \rangle$ with probability 1.

Both of these assertions are special cases of the following theorem: Let us generalize the concept of a complete algorithm. Let Ψ be a nondecreasing function of a natural argument, and let $\Psi(n) \to \infty$ for $n \to \infty$. We say that $\mathscr{P}$ is a Ψ-*complete* algorithm if the completeness condition holds for all k not exceeding $\Psi(l + 1)$. In other words, $\mathscr{P}$ is Ψ-complete if the zeros forbidden in the definition of completeness can appear only in the last $l + 1 - \Psi(l + 1)$ columns of $\{r_{ks}(\xi)\}$. Under the assumption $\Psi(n) \geqslant n$, the concepts of completeness and Ψ-completeness coincide; obviously, a complete algorithm is Ψ-complete for every Ψ.

We say that $\mathscr{P}$ is a *uniform algorithm* if there exists a constant C such that for every ξ all nonzero elements of $\{r_{ks}(\xi)\}$ exceed $C(i+1)^{-1}$ (for an equiprobabilistic algorithm, all nonzero elements are not less than $1/(l+1)m$).

THEOREM ON THE COMPLETENESS OF PROBABILISTIC DERIVATION   For any K, any word R derivable in K, any function Ψ, and any Ψ-complete algorithm $\mathscr{P}$, the probability $p[R]$ of the derivability of R in $\langle K, \mathscr{P} \rangle$ is different from zero. If, *in addition,* $\mathscr{P}$ is uniform and prohibits derivation cutoff, then $p[R] = 1$.

Extension to rules with more than one premise and the possibly non-unique result of application requires no essential changes but makes things more cumbersome. The essence of the necessary changes can be explained as follows.

For every canonical calculus K and every derivation B in it, the finite set of possible results of a single application of a rule of K to a word in B can always be enumerated (for instance, lexicographically). Now, algorithms can be introduced that assign to every B probabilities of its continuations, and terms such as "Ψ-complete," "uniform," and "prohibiting derivation cutoff" can be extended to this concept. In doing so, we can relate the parameter $l+1$ from the definition of uniformity to the length of B; and, because the number of possible continuations may far exceed that length, the complete equiprobabilistic algorithm can fail to be uniform! Or, to say it better, the rate of decrease of the probability of each particular derivation for an equiprobabilistic algorithm may be greater than $C/(l+1)$. This is why it is necessary to use Ψ-completeness, which permits introducing as many zeros as needed to guarantee that the nonzero elements decrease as $C/(l+1)$.

EXAMPLE 12   Consider the calculus

$$\{\{a, b\}, \{q_1, q_2\}, \{ab\}, \{q_1, q_2 \vdash aq_1 q_2 b\}\}.$$

Any derivation B of length l without repetitions has exactly l^2 possible continuations. But $l - 1$ of these continuations already belong to B. Hence the number of continuations of B that have no repetitions is $l^2 - l + 1$. Accordingly, the best complete equiprobabilistic algorithm for this calculus gives $l^2 - l + 1$ nonzero elements; consequently, each of them equals $(l^2 - l + 1)^{-1}$. The word *aababb* is derivable in this probabilistic calculus with

probability 1, whereas the probability that the derivable word *aabaababbb*
will not be derived is

$$\prod_{n=2}^{\infty} \frac{n^2 - n}{n^2 - n + 1} > \frac{2}{3} \prod_{k=2}^{\infty} \frac{k^2 - 1}{k^2} = \frac{1}{3}.$$

Consider now $\Psi(n) = \sqrt{n}$, and let us try to construct the best Ψ-complete
algorithm $\mathscr{P}$. Order all words in $\{a, b\}$ by length, and order words of the
same length lexicographically. Consider a derivation B of length l that has
no repetitions and consists of l "smallest" derivable words. The number of
its possible continuations is $n = l^2$. The algorithm $\mathscr{P}$ has the right to assign
probability 0 to each of these continuations except for the $\sqrt{n}$ smallest.
Among the remaining continuations, $l - 1$ are already in B (these are all
words from B except for the axiom). As a result, a $\sqrt{n}$-complete algorithm
has the right to assign 0 to all possible continuations except for one, namely,
the smallest continuation that is not in B. But then it is possible to assign
probability 1 to this continuation. Hence we arrive at a probabilistic
calculus in which the derivation process is deterministic! Each derivable
word will appear in its place with probability 1.

For this more general concept of a probabilistic calculus, the set of words
derivable with a probability greater than a given one is, again, r.e. If the
relevant concepts are defined in a proper way then the completeness theorem also holds.

Of special interest to later discussions are probabilistic calculi with
one-premise rules and an incomplete algorithm that allows the rules to
be applied only to the last word in the derivation. Here is a convenient
representation of such calculi, which uses the terminology of section 6.1.

A probabilistic system is any triple

$$\langle \mathscr{A}, Q_0, \mathscr{P} \rangle,$$

where Q_0 is the initial state of the system, $\mathscr{A}$ is its functioning algorithm,
and $\mathscr{P}$ is an algorithm applicable to every state Q. If $A(Q) = Q_1, \ldots, Q_f$, then

$$\mathscr{P}(Q) = p_0, p_1, \ldots, p_f, p_{\text{halt}} \qquad (4.2)$$

(all these numbers are nonnegative, $p_{\text{halt}} + \sum_{i=1}^{f} p_i = 1$). Here p_i is interpreted as the probability of moving to state Q_i ($1 \le i \le f$), p_{halt} as the
probability of a derivation cutoff (we also think of it as the probability of
moving to a special state, "halt"). In a similar way, we can consider the case
when $A(Q)$ is infinite, provided that the series in question converges to 1.

Readers familiar with the theory of probability will see that this probabilistic system is a Markov chain whose states are the objects derivable
in the calculus.

Problems

1. Compute the probability of deriving $|^{\langle 6 \rangle}$ in the calculus of example 11.

2. Construct the best equiprobabilistic ($\sqrt{n}+1$)-complete algorithm for
the calculus of example 12. For the algorithm of that probabilistic calculus,
compute (a) the probability of deriving *aabaababbb* and (b) the probability
of deriving that word by derivations of length 3 and length 4.

3. Prove the theorem on the completeness of probabilistic derivation.

4.2 Deductive Information

The more difficult it is to predict the state of the system after a certain
period of time, the more freedom of choice the system has. Thus we are
talking about the "indeterminacy" of the set of derivable states. When a set
is given and the probability of the appearance of each of its elements is
specified, the indeterminacy can be given a precise numeric characterization; this is done in information theory. The unit used in this characterization is the indeterminacy of the set of two elements that are assigned equal
probabilities. To find out which of the elements has appeared, it is necessary
to ask exactly one yes/no question. In the general case, indeterminacy
is measured by the number of yes/no questions necessary to specify the
element, for the most economical set of questions.

EXAMPLE 13   To find a number selected with equal probabilities from
among $\{1,2,\ldots,8\}$, one has to answer all three of the following questions:
(1) Is $X \leqslant 4$? If the answer is no, then (2) Is X in $\{5,6\}$? (Otherwise (2) Is
X in $\{1,2\}$?) The last question is obvious. It is clear that, in case the probabilities are equal, the indeterminacy of the set $\{1,2,\ldots,2^n\}$ is n.

EXAMPLE 14   Consider the set $\{1,2,3,4\}$. Let the probabilities of the ap-
pearance of the elements be $\frac{1}{8},\frac{1}{8},\frac{1}{4},\frac{1}{2}$. Example 13 shows that two questions
would suffice. But this method is not the most economical. As a matter of
fact, the following sequence of questions is somewhat more advantageous:
(1) Is $X = 4$? If not, then (2) Is $X = 3$? If not, then (3) Is $X = 2$? Even though,

in two cases, this sequence requires three questions, the expectation of the number of questions is less than 2:

$$3 \times \tfrac{1}{8} + 3 \times \tfrac{1}{8} + 2 \times \tfrac{1}{4} + 1 \times \tfrac{1}{2} = 1\tfrac{3}{4}.$$

In the general case of an n-element set with probabilities $p_1, \ldots, p_n$, indeterminacy of the set, or *entropy*, or the *information* needed for removing this indeterminacy, is computed according to the formula

$$H = -\sum_{i=1}^{n} p_i \log_2 p_i. \tag{4.3}$$

In example 13, for instance, we get

$$\sum_{i=1}^{2^n} \frac{1}{2^n} \times \log_2 2^n = n.$$

Formula (4.3) extends also to the case of $n = \infty$.

Let us go back now to probabilistic calculus (4.2) from section 4.1. Let $\langle A, Q_0 \rangle \vdash Q$ mean that Q is derivable in $\langle A, Q_0 \rangle$; let p_Q be the probability that the derivation will stop in state Q (that is, that Q is the last state before the derivation terminates). Taking into account that we can arrive at Q by different paths, we should compute p_Q for *all possible* derivations that end in Q. Let the *information* in (4.2) be the function

$$I_{\langle A, Q_0, \mathscr{P} \rangle} = -\sum_{Q \in \langle A, Q_0 \rangle} p_Q \log_2 p_Q. \tag{4.4}$$

This function depends on both the calculus and the probabilistic measure $\mathscr{P}$. We are interested in the informational properties of $\langle A, Q_0 \rangle$ itself, as far as possible independently of $\mathscr{P}$. To study the "power" of $\langle A, Q_0 \rangle$ (the number of states derived in unit time), let us standardize $\mathscr{P}$.

Let us fix the probability p of cutoff at each step of the derivation ($p > 0, q = 1 - p$). In other words, for every Q, $\mathscr{P}(Q)$ gives the same probability p_{halt} ($p_{\text{halt}} = p$). If Q is a dead-end state, then $\mathscr{P}(Q) = q$ (that is, $p_0 = q$). In addition, let $\mathscr{P}$ assign equal probabilities to all possible destinations (that is, if Q is not a dead-end state, then $p_0 = 0, p_1 = p_2 = \ldots = p_l = q/l$). When $\mathscr{P}$ has been fixed in such a way, function (4.4) becomes a function of p; we call it *information* in $\langle A, Q_0 \rangle$ and denote it by $I_{\langle A, Q_0 \rangle}(p)$.

Intuitively, the concept of information in a calculus reflects to what degree the process of derivation in this calculus can branch. If the probability p of cutoff is large, then, in estimating the branching of the process here, we take into account only the first two or three steps of the work of the system. But if p is small, then we examine larger segments of the possible ways of functioning.

Thus p describes the average length of the trajectories to be examined, and the behavior of $I_S(p)$ for $p \to 0$ is the most important characteristic of the indeterminacy inherent in a calculus S. The following theorem can be proved.

THEOREM ON THE ASYMPTOTICS OF INFORMATION   If only finitely many states are derivable in S, then $I_S(p)$ is a bounded function. If S is infinite and deterministic (that is, has no branches), then, for $p \to 0$, $I_S(p)$ tends to infinity as $|\log_2 p|$. If for some L every derivation in S has at most L continuations (all k-local calculi and TP-calculi satisfy this condition), then $I_S(p) < c/p$. If S is any canonical calculus, then $I_S(p) < c/p^2$.

This theorem demonstrates the different rates at which information approaches infinity for different types of branching. All the assertions together show that the concept of information conforms sufficiently well to intuition and, in particular, can serve as a formalization of the idea of *freedom of economic choice* (see chapter 6). The concept of information I have introduced also has other applications, in particular, to biology (chapter 7).

Problems

1. Calculate the entropy of a countable set with the probabilities of elements equal to $\frac{1}{2}, \frac{1}{4}, \frac{1}{8} \ldots$.

2. Calculate $I_D(p)$, where D is an infinite deterministic calculus. (First consider the case $p = \frac{1}{2}$).

II Horizontal Modeling

By your gentle and shy shoe,
Subdue distance by feet!
M. Tsvetaeva

5 A Toy Economy

A huge number of precisely investigated facts and phenomena are available. By applying to them logical methods of work ... science gradually explains, extends and builds its world-view. But ...

V. I. Vernadsky

It would have been so easy,
If it weren't so very hard!

Yu. Levitansky

This chapter deals with simple models of economic systems. Despite their simplicity, it is possible to reflect in them, besides purely technological aspects of economic systems, their functioning as systems with control, information processing, and such. In the next chapter the models are made more substantial, and qualitative conclusions are drawn from their analysis. I do not give here a complete description of economic aspects of the concepts and results of these two chapters; these aspects can be reconstructed by the reader in the framework of the theory of economic systems (see, for instance, [21]).

5.1 Stable Economic Systems

The concept of a k-local calculus provides a natural formalization of the concept of a stable economic system (SES). Assume a fixed number of *control centers* (CCs), a possible set of resources and products circulating in the system, and a set of possible transformations of the resources as a result of joint or separate actions of the CCs. Then the current state of the system is described by specifying the *list of resources* (LR) that each CC has available at a given time. Enumerate all CCs (let there be N of them) and all resources and products (say, h in number). We view all resources and products as discrete so that their quantities are measured by natural numbers. Now we can construct, in an obvious way, a k-local calculus (with $K = Nh - 1$) whose derivations completely describe the functioning of the SES. The current state of the SES is represented by a word of the form

$$1^{\langle l_{11}\rangle}\Box 1^{\langle l_{12}\rangle}\ldots\Box 1^{\langle l_{1h}\rangle}\Box\ldots\Box 1^{\langle l_{N1}\rangle}\Box 1^{\langle l_{N2}\rangle}\ldots\Box 1^{\langle l_{Nh}\rangle}, \tag{5.1}$$

where l_{ij} stands for the number of units of the ith resource (or product) in the LR of the ith CC. Any transformation of resources, whether it consists in producing something or in an exchange between CCs, can easily be described by an appropriate rule of the form

$$\frac{1^{\langle l_0 \rangle} p_0 \square 1^{\langle l_1 \rangle} p_1 \square \ldots \square 1^{\langle l_k \rangle} p_k}{1^{\langle l_0 \rangle} p_0 \square 1^{\langle l_1 \rangle} p_1 \square \ldots \square 1^{\langle l_k \rangle} p_k}. \tag{$*$}$$

For instance, assume that $h = 3$ and that there exists the following techno-logical possibility of interaction between CC^1 and CC^2: 4 units of resource 3 of CC^1 and 3 units of resource 1 of CC^2 can be transformed into 2 units of resource (or product) 2, which will be controlled by CC^2. This possibility should be represented by the rule

$$\frac{p_1 \square p_2 \square 1111 p_3 \square 111 p_4 \square p_5 \square p_6 \square \ldots \square p_{Nh}}{p_1 \square p_2 \square p_3 \square p_4 \square 11 p_5 \square p_6 \square \ldots \square p_{Nh}}. \tag{5.2}$$

The initial state of the SES is described by a word of form (5.1) and is taken to be the axiom; the possible ways of functioning for this initial state are described by various derivations in the constructed calculus. (Notice that in reality it is not necessary to take $k = Nh - 1$; usually it is obvious that some resources cannot possibly come under control of a given CC, and we do not have to assign special places between squares to the corresponding "constant zeros.")

Let us consider now some types of *TP-rules* (rules of technological possibilities) and abbreviated notation for them. Usually, a TP depends on the activity of one or two, or at most three different CCs. Consequently, the notation for rules of interaction that specifies the CCs to which the rule applies and the resources affected by the rule will be much more efficient than rule (5.2). To this end, each of the h resources can be denoted by a special letter from the alphabet

$$\{a_1, a_2, \ldots, a_h\}, \tag{5.3}$$

and three inference rules are written as follows.

1. A TP of a fixed CC is described in the form

$$CC^\alpha: \frac{k_1 a_{i_1}, \ldots, k_r a_{i_r}}{k_1' a_{j_1}, \ldots, k_{r'}' a_{j_{r'}}} \tag{5.4}$$

and denotes the possibility of transforming k_1 units of resource $a_{i_1}, \ldots, k_r$ units of resource a_{i_r} into as many units of each of the resources $a_{j_1}, \ldots, a_{j_{r'}}$, as shown below the bar. (That is, the resources shown above the bar are deleted from the LR of CC^α, and the resources shown below the bar are added to it.) The rule is applicable, of course, only if the LR of CC^α contains the required quantities of resources.

EXAMPLE 4 (continued from chapter 1)   The system consists of one CC; take the alphabet $\{m_1, m_2, n_1, n_2, n_3\}$ as alphabet (5.3). The second and the sixth inference rules can be written now in the abbreviated form

$$CC^1 : \frac{m_1}{n_2, n_3}, \quad CC^1 : \frac{m_2}{n_2, 2n_3}$$

(that is, we get the most straightforward notation for possible ways of cutting).

2. We represent a *rule of interaction* between CC^α and CC^β in the form

$$CC^\alpha - CC^\beta : \frac{k_1 a_{i_1}, \ldots, k_r a_{i_r} \square k_{r+1} a_{j_1}, \ldots, k_{r+R} a_{j_R}}{k'_1 a_{f_1}, \ldots, k'_{r'} a_{f_{r'}} \square k_{r'+1} a_{g_1}, \ldots, k_{r'+R'} a_{g_{R'}}} \qquad (5.5)$$

with the obvious meaning. For instance,

$$CC^1 - CC^2 : \frac{10 a_1 \square 3 a_4}{3 a_4 \square 10 a_1}$$

means that 10 units of resource 1 should be taken from the LR of CC^1 and 3 units of resource 4 should be added to it and that the LR of CC^2 should be changed in the opposite way. Such a rule is an exchange rule; rules with the "exhaustion" of some resource are also natural. For instance,

$$CC^1 - CC^2 : \frac{12 a_1 \square 3 a_4}{3 a_4 \square 10 a_1} \qquad (5.6)$$

means that CC^1 had to pay 2 units of resource 1 for the exchange (say, 3 units of resource 4 cost 10 rubles, and 2 rubles is the cost of transportation).

The form of rule (5.5) provides for both the possibility of various exchanges and the possibility of the emergence of new resources or the increase of the total quantity of the old resources resulting from interaction between CC^α and CC^β. These types of rules can easily be distinguished in a formal way: If the condition

$$\forall i \, (1 \leqslant i \leqslant h \Rightarrow ((i = i_\varepsilon = j_\zeta = f_\gamma = g_\delta) \Rightarrow k_\varepsilon + k_{r+\zeta} \geqslant k'_\gamma + k'_{r'+\delta})) \qquad (5.7)$$

is satisfied, then we have an exchange rule with exhaustion; if the condition obtained by substituting $=$ in condition (5.7) for $\geqslant$ holds, then we have a rule of "pure exchange." If condition (5.7) is violated for at least one resource, then we say that we are dealing with a rule of *proper interaction*. (It is assumed that $k = 0$ for each resource not shown in rule (5.5) explicitly.)

3. A natural rule whose operation affects more than two CCs models the activity of a transportation agency, a salesperson, etc. We get an example of such a rule if in rule (5.6) we explicitly mention the agent who is paid for transportation. This rule may look like

$$CC^1 - CC^2 - CC^3 : \frac{12a_1 \square 3a_4 \square a_5}{3a_4 \square 10a_1 \square 2a_1, \, a_5}, \tag{5.8}$$

and its interpretation is obvious: CC^1 bought 3 units of resource 4 for 10 rubles and paid 2 rubles to the transportation agency CC^3 for transportation; to be able to carry out transportation, CC^3 must have at least one unit of resource 5 at its disposal (say, a truck), which remains under its control after use.

Comparing rule (5.6) with rule (5.8) helps us to understand the principles of decomposing more complex systems into simpler ones. If we are not interested in the functioning and structure of the transportation agency and if we have to control a system in which only the cost of transportation is essential, then we should eliminate CC^3 and use rule (5.6). If, on the other hand, we are interested in controlling the transportation agency, then we should use a detailed description of the structure of CC^3 and redundant information about external customers should be removed from the description of the system. (In other words, we should delete to some degree CC^1 and CC^2 from the description; it may be irrelevant, for instance, that the cost of the purchase was 10 rubles.) But, generally, the description of an SES may require rules of type (5.8) and even more complex rules, including an even greater number of CCs. Notice that, in the spirit of the definitions given above, it is natural to view rule (5.8) as a rule of pure exchange.

These examples show that the description of real-life economic systems in the form of appropriate calculi is practically impossible: The calculi are too bulky. Consequently, the apparatus of deductive systems cannot yet handle a precise quantitative analysis of a situation; however, this apparatus is well developed for the study of qualitative properties of calculi, which allows us to arrive at qualitative conclusions of an economic nature. Consider, for instance, a natural economic problem: Given the current state of the system, determine whether it is possible to organize its functioning so as to achieve a given desirable state. This problem turns out to be the standard mathematical problem of deciding whether a given object can be derived in a given calculus. It becomes possible, then, to compare different forms of control on the basis of differences between the deductive possibilities of corresponding calculi.

It is important to observe in this connection that the reformulation of the rules just discussed (and even more complex rules involving many CCs) in terms of k-local calculi always gives a rule of form (∗). Similarly, in the other direction, given a rule of form (∗), it is easy to figure out which CCs are actually affected by it and how to describe it in abbreviated notation. For instance, rule (5.2), obviously, can be written in the form

$$CC^1 - CC^2 : \frac{4a_3 \square 3a_4}{\square 2a_2}.$$

So the study of properties of various SESs in this sense reduces to the study of one mathematical concept, k-local calculi.

5.2 Supervisors and Subordinates: Technological and Economic Systems

Using the concepts introduced, we can describe not only the functioning of rigid technological systems involved in the production and exchange of material resources and products but also the work of much more flexible systems, in which "informational resources" are processed, economic decisions are made, relations between managers and subordinates are essential, etc. Let us begin with technological systems.

Consider first an isolated CC. For instance, let this CC be a supervisor who has to deal with a cutting problem. On the one hand, the supervisor is a control center of a sufficiently complex system that consists of workers with different abilities and qualifications. This means that the supervisor has to solve a number of completely nontechnological problems. On the other hand, the supervisor is a part of a large system, and from the point of view of that system the supervisor's department is a single CC^1 with fixed TPs. This separation of two levels is a perfectly adequate method of approximate analysis of an economic system. From the viewpoint of the large system, such possibilities as the possibility of rearranging the work force are invisible, and only purely technological possibilities, which coincide with various ways of cutting and are formalized in section 5.1 by rules of form (5.4), can be expressed. From this external point of view, the actions of CC^1 should be optimized relative to the chosen goal (which should be known, of course, both to the system and to the supervisor). After that, it can be assumed that the result of the operation of this CC is completely determined by the resources (and by the goal, that is, by the working assignment) that are given to it. At the level of precision accepted here, this means that CC^1 fails to be a center performing control. In other words, it can be deleted from the description of the SES altogether. It becomes unnecessary to consider its own TPs. Formally, the activity of the SES is replaced by "global" TP-rules related to some CC^2: This is the CC delivering materials to the supervisor. Instead of the rule actually present in the system of transferring materials to CC^1 (and receiving the finished products from it), CC^2 should be given a rule for seemingly direct transformation of materials into products.

On the one hand, this example shows that the usual problems of mathematical economics can be reformulated in the language selected here and are therefore special cases of problems for studying SESs. Consequently, the available mathematical apparatus (primarily the methods of integer programming) may serve as a partial foundation of the theory of SESs under the approach proposed here. On the other hand, the example shows how the solution of problems of mathematical programming can be used for simplifying an SES and for exposing its economic part proper. "Raising" TPs from CC^1 to CC^2 demonstrated in this example can be systematically performed for any SES, and, consequently, it makes it possible, in principle, to delete the technological part of the system and to consider all decisions on the level on which there is no unique goal, goals are yet to be separated from restrictions, etc.

Let us now try to distinguish technological from "supertechnological" systems by looking at whether they include resources that are informational by nature. It is difficult to define a formal distinction between informational and material resources; an adequate approach should be based on the meaning of the given SES rather than on its form. For most SESs, however, one can use the property of being easily acquired as a good formal approximation to the concept of informational resources. The precise formulation of this property is given in chapter 6, section 6.2; meanwhile, the following simple definition will do. A resource a_i is called *informational* if a rule of the form

$$CC^\alpha: \frac{\cdot}{a_i} \qquad\qquad\qquad (5.9)$$

is available in the SES, that is, if the resource can be obtained "free of charge."

Let us look at a few ways to use informational resources in SESs. The formalization accepted in the foregoing discussion is based on the assumption that a rule is applicable as soon as the CCs mentioned in the rule have at their disposal the resources required by the rule (that is, when they are included in the premise). It appears, then, that a condition such as the willingness of a certain CC to share information is not stipulated here. Similarly, if a rule affects only one CC, then its applicability seems to be independent of anyone's permission. For purely technological systems this understanding of applicability is natural; if the application of a given TP is possible and expedient from the viewpoint of a unique goal (which is the same for all CCs of the system), then how can different CCs possibly have any conflicting desires? This discussion shows that the specifically economic character of the system is largely connected with the structure of permissions and orders concerning the application of various TPs.

This structure can easily be expressed in terms of the concepts proposed here. Adding this structure to a purely technological scheme requires that informational resources be introduced and that the form of rules be changed; but from the mathematical viewpoint the modified system is an object of exactly the same type as the initial one. When the system is described as a k-local calculus, the value of k increases, but the rules still have the form $(*)$. The idea of transforming a technological SES into an SES with permissions and orders is explained by a few examples.

EXAMPLE 15   Consider an exchange rule

$$CC^1 - CC^2 : \frac{k_1 a_1 \square k_2 a_2}{k_2 a_2 \square k_1 a_1} \tag{5.10}$$

with an additional stipulation: We want its applicability to depend on the consent of CC^1. To denote the "consent to exchange," introduce a new resource (formally, extend the alphabet of resources (5.3) by a new letter, a_{h+1}). For this resource we add a rule of form (5.9):

$$CC^1 : \frac{\cdot}{a_{h+1}},$$

and replace (5.10) by the rule

$$CC^1 - CC^2 : \frac{k_1 a_1, \, a_{h+1} \square k_2 a_2}{k_2 a_2 \square k_1 a_1}. \tag{5.11}$$

Now CC^2 cannot perform the exchange at will; it has to wait until CC^1 produces the permission a_{h+1}. In this rule we deal with a one-time permission (for every new exchange, a_{h+1} has to be produced again). It is no more difficult to model the "permanent agreement," that is, the existence of a long-term contract. The corresponding rule has the form

$$CC^1 - CC^2 : \frac{k_1 a_1, \, a_{h+1} \square k_2 a_2}{k_2 a_2, \, a_{h+1} \square k_1 a_1}$$

(that is, resource a_{h+1} is not exhausted, and any number of exchanges like this can be performed). An application of this rule can be viewed as transforming the system with rule (5.11) into a system in which the consent of CC^1 is no longer needed; that is, we can go back to the less cumbersome system with rule (5.10).

EXAMPLE 16   Assume that CC^1 has rule (5.4), and let us model the fact that CC^1 has the right to use this rule only with permission of CC^2. Let us use the same method of extending alphabet (5.3) by a new informational resource a_{h+1}. Add the rules

$$CC^2 : \frac{\cdot}{a_{h+1}}, \quad CC^1 - CC^2 : \frac{\square a_{h+1}}{a_{h+1} \square}.$$

Rule (5.4) is changed in the obvious way:

$$CC^\alpha : \frac{k_1 a_{i_1}, \ldots, k_r a_{i_r}, \, a_{h+1}}{k'_1 a_{j_1}, \ldots, k'_{r'} a_{j_{r'}}}.$$

Now CC^1 can use the given "exchange" rule, but not until CC^2 produces at least one letter a_{h+1}. So TP (5.4) cannot be applied until a permission is granted in CC^2. The case when this permission is of long-term nature, rather than for one time use, can be taken into account as was done in example 15 (and here again it is more convenient to return to rule (5.4)).

EXAMPLE 17   Let CC^1 and CC^2 be able to do the same work, but what they do depends on the work place assigned to each of them. Let CC^3 be the manager. Let work place 1 be associated with possibilities P_1 and P_2, and work place 2 with possibilities P_3 and P_4. We add two letters a_{h+1}, a_{h+2}

to the alphabet and introduce the rules

$$CC^3: \frac{\cdot}{a_{h+1}}, \quad CC^3: \frac{\cdot}{a_{h+2}}, \quad CC^1 - CC^3: \frac{\Box a_{h+1}}{a_{h+1}\Box}, \quad CC^1 - CC^3: \frac{\Box a_{h+2}}{a_{h+2}\Box},$$

$$CC^2 - CC^3: \frac{\Box a_{h+1}}{a_{h+1}\Box}, \quad CC^2 - CC^3: \frac{\Box a_{h+2}}{a_{h+2}\Box}.$$

We introduce P_1 and P_2, with a_{h+1} included in the premises, and P_3 and P_4, with a_{h+2} added, in the list of TPs belonging to CC^1. CC^2 is handled in a similar way but with a_{h+1} and a_{h+2} interchanged. Now, to assign work places to the workers, CC^3 should produce either two units of a_{h+1} or two units of a_{h+2}. The work of CC^3 in the case when it can assign the same work place to both CC^1 and CC^2 is modeled in a similar manner.

These examples show how "nontechnological" decisions can be modeled in the language of SESs; sufficiently complex economic decisions can be modeled on the basis of the same ideas. In principle, this apparatus is capable of formally describing the "day-to-day" operation of a typical economic system (without emergencies and global changes and decisions that are particularly difficult to foresee). It is convenient to use some abbreviations and symbols in such descriptions (such as arrows for expressing subordination), but such details are of no significance for qualitative modeling. Global changes and methods of changing the set of TPs are discussed in section 5.3.

5.3   Systems without Stability

It is possible to introduce in the terms various generalizations of SESs connected with the loss of stability (one by one or all at once). In this section I consider generalizations of three kinds that do not require substantial extension of the mathematical apparatus: (1) changing the list of TP-rules without changing the structure of the CCs and connections between them; (2) changing connections between the CCs; and (3) changing the list of CCs (see chapter 6 for further generalizations).

An unlimited extension of the list of TPs is a simple and at the same time significant form of generalization. Formally, a list of TP-rules is given as a sequence of rules (which can be arbitrarily long). Here the conditions of applicability of the rules (consisting in specifying certain resources in premises) allow us to extend gradually the set of applicable rules in the course of generation of appropriate resources in the system, as in a typical SES. In actually organizing the process of introducing new rules, we should use informational resources (as in section 5.2). For instance, the "discovery" of a new TP should be modeled as the permission to use it. (That is, some CC, interpreted as a research institute or as a license-purchasing department, produces the resource a_{h+1}, which is passed in the process of exchange to the interested CCs. The new TP-rule should have a_{h+1} among its premises. Incidentally, by passing a_{h+1} in exchange for some informational resource produced earlier, we can model a ban on the use of old technology.) If the new technology is associated with the introduction of a new material resource (in which "the discovery is materialized"), then that resource itself plays the role of "permission."

Practically, of course, it is inconvenient to view all TP-rules as potentially present in the system from the beginning. Notice that the problem of optimization of the operation of the system can be solved only when sufficiently complete information is available about the "planned" technology that has not yet been "discovered" (in the most obvious case, we decide whether we should acquire and add to our TPs something well known). In other words, it is possible to optimize work only when the system is fairly close to stability.

So far I have not specified whether new TP-rules involve connections between sets of CCs that were not connected before. In the general case, we deal with changing the structure of connections.

Changing the Structure of Connections

I consider in this context only one special problem: Given a fixed set of CCs, with their LRs and TPs (not interaction rules), determine which exchange connections should be added.

In what follows I assume that the system satisfies the monotonicity condition: Any TP-rule applicable for fixed LRs will remain applicable if the LRs in the CCs affected by this rule do not decrease. (By $LR_1 \leqslant LR_2$ I mean that the inequality is satisfied for each resource on the lists.) When the system is specified by rules (5.4), (5.5), (5.8), and the like, the monotonicity condition is obviously satisfied (but for arbitrary k-local calculi it can be violated). For a more detailed analysis of this condition, see section 5.8.

For a fixed current state of the system $S(t)$, denote the union of all LRs of all CCs in this state by $LR_{S(t)}$. Let the sequence of applications of

TP-rules in the system be written as $S(0), \ldots, S(t)$. The *trace* of this functioning is the list

$$\mathrm{LR}_{S(0)}, \mathrm{LR}_{S(1)}, \ldots, \mathrm{LR}_{S(t)}. \tag{5.12}$$

We say that a system S' *functions no worse than* S if for every trace (5.12) one can find a trace

$$\mathrm{LR}_{S'(0)}, \mathrm{LR}_{S'(1)}, \ldots, \mathrm{LR}_{S'(t')}$$

such that $\mathrm{LR}_{S'(0)} = \mathrm{LR}_{S'(0)}$, $\mathrm{LR}_{S'(t')} \leqslant \mathrm{LR}_{S(t)}$, and $t' \leqslant t$. By induction on the length of the trace we can easily prove the following lemma.

LEMMA 1   If the set of TP-rules and LRs of CC^1 is contained in the set of TP-rules and LRs of CC^2, then in this situation the system in which exchanges are forbidden between CC^1 and CC^2 functions no worse than the system in which they are permitted. If this relationship between CC^1 and CC^2 is violated, then a system can always be constructed whose functioning requires exchanges between CC^1 and CC^2.

The lemma exhibits one trivial case when one can do without a connection between CC^1 and CC^2. A less trivial situation when exchanges of a certain form are not needed is described in the following lemma.

LEMMA 2   For any system S one can construct a system S' that functions no worse than S, in which a CC never receives as a result of an exchange any resource that does not occur in the premises of its TP-rules.

It should be observed, however, that the construction of S' may possibly involve the loss of equivalent exchange. That is, S' demonstrates both the advantages and the disadvantages of a natural economy. In connection with that, consider example 18.

EXAMPLE 18   A system S has CCs with the rules

$$CC^1 : \frac{3c}{10a}, \quad CC^2 : \frac{10a}{b}, \quad CC^3 : \frac{b}{4c}. \tag{5.13}$$

Let exchanges in S be organized on the principle of sale, with the universal resource denoted by r. More specifically, let $a = 1r$, $c = 3r$, $b = 11r$; that is, one of the exchange rules is

$$CC^1 - CC^2 : \frac{3r \square c}{c \square 3r}.$$

System S' is obtained by simply deleting all occurrences of the resources not occurring in rules (5.13); that is, the exchange becomes

$$CC^1 - CC^2 : \frac{\square c}{c \square}.$$

An attempt to preserve equivalent exchange without including any resources not transformed inside a CC in that CC (such as b and r in CC^1) leads to the cumbersome rule of triple exchange:

$$CC^1 - CC^2 - CC^3 : \frac{33a \square 3b \square 11c}{11c \square 33a \square 3b}.$$

The resulting system S'' may function no worse than the initial one, but not for all initial data.

Questions of this sort are also related to the problem of defining formally the complexity of an economic system. Let n be the total number of CCs in the system, and let k be the maximal possible number of meaningful connections between pairs of CCs (that is, connections for which it makes sense to organize exchanges); k can be calculated, for instance, as in lemma 1. Define the *normalized complexity* of the system to be the number $k/\binom{n}{2}$. Obviously, normalized complexity is between 0 and 1. Incidentally, k depends on the current state. Define the complexity of the system to be k/n.

LEMMA 3   Let S_2 be obtained from S_1 by adding one CC that can be connected by exchanges with exactly l old CCs; let the normalized complexity of S_1 be α, and let its complexity be β; also, let the number of CCs in S_1 be n. Then the normalized complexity of S_2 will be greater than, less than, or equal to α, depending on whether $l/n > \alpha$, $l/n < \alpha$, or $l/n = \alpha$. Similarly, the complexity of S_2 will be greater than, less than, or equal to β, depending on whether $l > \beta$, $l < \beta$, or $l = \beta$.

The complexity may go up even when the normalized complexity goes down. Lemma 3 allows us to estimate the change of an SES as a whole on the basis of its local change.

So far as the changes in the set of CCs are concerned, the most interesting of them are splitting and merging CCs (with the partial splitting and merging of their TPs). The following three transformations correspond to merging two CCs in the system: (1) combining LRs, (2) assigning the same number to the merged CCs in the descriptions of CC rules, (3) combining the resources related to the merging CCs in the premises and conclusions of those TP-rules whose descriptions include both CCs. For instance, merging CC^1 and CC^3 in rule (5.8) gives the rule

$$CC^1 - CC^2 : \frac{12a_1, a_5 \square 3a_4}{2a_1, 3a_4, a_5 \square 10a_1}.$$

Here again we assume the monotonicity condition.

LEMMA 4   After merging CCs, the system functions no worse than before.

Merging can be used to produce eventually a system with just one CC. In particular, the following lemma holds.

LEMMA 5   If all interaction rules in S are exchanges, then the system that consists of one CC with all rules of S of form (5.4) assigned to it and with the list of resources equal to $LR_{S(0)}$ function no worse than $S(0)$.

Problems

1.   Write a calculus that is similar to that of example 6 but allows the assignment of the same work place to both workers.

2.   Model a technological possibility affecting three CCs that can be used when the decision is made by the majority of the CCs.

3.   For which initial data can systems S, S', and S'' from example 18 function for an infinitely long time?

6 Calculi of Technological Possibilities

The language of the theory of algorithms allows us to reformulate the notion of a deductive system. The new definition is much more general than the previous one and allows richer interpretations.

6.1 TP-Calculi and Their Algorithmic Properties

Let n be a positive integer. $(n + 1)$-ary vectors with positive integer coordinates are called states. Let A be an algorithm that takes an arbitrary state as its input and returns a finite list of states. ($Q' \in A(Q)$ means that Q' belongs to $A(Q)$.) Consider a pair (A, Q_0), where Q_0 is a state called the initial state and A is called the algorithm of functioning for the system (A, Q_0). A should be viewed as a generalized rule of inference that defines the following relation of immediate derivability:

$$Q \vdash Q' \leftrightarrow Q' \in A(Q).$$

The previous definitions can be viewed as a definition of a deductive system with the axiom Q_0 and the inference rule A.

We say that the system can move from a state Q_1 to a state Q_2 if Q_2 is derivable in calculus (A, Q_1). The first component of a state is called the system's *mode*, and n other components, the system's *resources*. A state Q such that $A(Q)$ is empty is called an *impasse state*. The relation $\geqslant$ on the set of states is defined as

$$(\alpha, X_1, \ldots, X_n) \geqslant (\beta, Y_1, \ldots, Y_n) \Leftrightarrow ((\alpha = \beta) \,\&\, \forall i (X_i \geqslant Y_i)).$$

We say that an algorithm A is monotonic if

$$\forall Q_1 Q_1' Q_2 ((Q_1 \vdash Q_1' \,\&\, Q_2 \geqslant Q_1) \Rightarrow \exists Q_2' (Q_2 \vdash Q_2' \,\&\, Q_2' \geqslant Q_1')) \qquad (6.1)$$

(that is, if the increase of resources cannot decrease the power of the system). A system (A, Q_0) such that A is monotonic and such that the set of the first components of states derivable in the system is bounded (that is, the system has a finite number of modes) is called a *TP-system*.

Economic systems with a finite number of modes such that in each mode there is a finite number of technological possibilities (which depends on the available resources) may serve as natural interpretations of TP-systems. From the point of view of this interpretation, the monotonicity condition is natural. On the other hand, in real economic systems the following *overregulation condition* can frequently be found: If a supplier S has a necessary resource, then that resource has to be bought from S. If such a rule is incorporated into the system, then it can lead to blocking some possibilities related to other suppliers and to the violation of the monotonicity condition for this system. There are some other reasons why the monotonicity condition fails (for example, those related to the cost of storage: The more resources stored, the less possible it is to use the same storage space), but all of them can be avoided by appropriately defining the corresponding TPs. (For example, the cost of storage can be included in the cost of production, or the storage space can be viewed as one of the resources to be processed.) The overregulation condition can also be abandoned (and replaced, for example, by fines). This transformation does not worsen the effectiveness of the operation of the system (as can be proved for different measures of effectiveness). At the same time, as I intend to show in this section, the analysis of the system's behavior and the search for the optimal control strategy are greatly simplified.

In some respects the language of TP-systems is too general. I put some restrictions on the algorithm of functioning to make it more suitable for economic interpretations. Let us define A by the number of modes N and a list of pairs $(\beta_\alpha^j, f_\alpha^j)$, where α and β_α^j are modes and f_α^j are production functions $(1 \leqslant j \leqslant l_\alpha)$ that map the n-dimensional space on itself and that do not decrease with respect to each argument. The result X of an application of A to a state α is the list of all states γ, β, Y such that

$$\exists_j (\beta = \beta_\alpha^j \;\&\; Y = [f_\alpha^j(X)] \;\&\; Y \geqslant 0). \tag{6.2}$$

(Here, $[Z]$ is a vector consisting of the integral parts of components of a vector Z. A can be applied to an arbitrary state and returns an l-member list, where $0 \leqslant l \leqslant l_\alpha$. l depends on X and is less than l_α because of those j for which $[f_\alpha^j(X)]$ contains negative components.) Such an explicit definition of A enumerates TP-systems by specifying production functions. The monotonicity of these functions is guaranteed by condition (6.1). (Some TP-systems cannot be defined in such form, but most likely they are not very interesting from the viewpoint of economic interpretations.)

We now need a property of algorithms of functioning, which we call *immediate decidability*. Let $Z_1, \ldots, Z_n$ be a list of positive integers and $K = (Z_1^{\varepsilon_1}, \ldots, Z_n^{\varepsilon_n})$, where $\forall i (\varepsilon_i \in \{=, \geqslant\})$, $(X_1, \ldots, X_n) \in K$ means $X_1 \varepsilon_1 Z_1$, $\ldots$, $X_n \varepsilon_n Z_n$ (K is a cone in n-dimensional space). An algorithm of functioning, algorithm A is immediately decidable if for any α, K, Q_1 it is possible to find X and Q_2 such that $X \in K$, $Q_2 \geqslant Q_1$ and α, X immediately derive Q_2. If our production functions are defined in a natural way, then A must be immediately decidable. We are interested in finding a state of the system that is not worse than our goal state (with repect to all parameters). To put it in more rigorous terms, consider the following property of TP-systems: the possibility to decide, given an arbitrary state Q_1 if there exists a derivable Q_2 such that $Q_2 \geqslant Q_1$. A TP-system that satisfies this property is called weakly decidable.

THEOREM 1   For any immediately decidable algorithm A and an arbitrary state Q_0, the TP-system (A, Q_0) is weakly decidable.

Proof   We outline the proof of the theorem for the case of only one mode and $n = 2$. The first condition is not really a restriction, as can be seen from the following lemma.

LEMMA   For any TP-system (A, Q_0) it is possible to find an enumeration of states (denoted by $K_{\lfloor \rfloor}$) and an algorithm A^K with one mode such that A^K is monotonic for all components and the TP-system $\langle A^K, K_{\lfloor}Q_0{\rfloor}\rangle$ derives codes of those and only those states that are derived in the initial system.

Let N be the number of modes of the initial system. We use an $(N + n + 1)$-ary vector

$$\underbrace{0, \ldots, 0,}_{\alpha+1 \text{ times}} I, \underbrace{0, \ldots, 0}_{N-\alpha \text{ times}} \qquad\qquad (6.3)$$

as the code of a state α, X.

If $A(Q) = Q_1, \ldots, Q_p$, then the result of applying A^K to $K_{\lfloor}Q{\rfloor}$ will be the list $K_{\lfloor}Q_1{\rfloor}, \ldots, K_{\lfloor}Q_p{\rfloor}$. The system $\langle A^K, K_{\lfloor}Q_0{\rfloor}\rangle$ completely models the work of the initial system; hence the only states derivable in it are the states of type (6.3). This allows us to define A^K arbitrarily for states other than type (6.3). In particular, we can use an extension that is monotonic.

The requirement $n = 2$ is introduced only to simplify the argument. Suppose that our goal is to check whether or not a state X'_1, X'_2, where $X'_1 \geqslant \bar{X}_1$, $X'_2 \geqslant \bar{X}_2$, is derivable in our system. Consider a cone $(\bar{X}_1 - 1^=, 0^\geqslant)$. Using the immediate decidability of A, we can check whether there is a state $\bar{X}_1 - 1, Y_2$ from which some goal X'_1, X'_2 can be immediately derived. If such an $\bar{X}_1 - 1, Y_2$ does not exist, then there is no other Y_1, Y_2 $(Y_1 < \bar{X}_1)$ from which X'_1, X'_2 can be derived in one step. If $\bar{X}_1 - 1, Y_2$ is found, then we can make the list

$$(\bar{X}_1, \bar{X}_2), (\bar{X}_1 - 1, Y_2). \qquad\qquad (6.4)$$

The states satisfying the disjunction

$$(X_1' \geqslant \bar{X}_1 \ \& \ X_2' \geqslant \bar{X}_2) \vee (X_1' \geqslant \bar{X}_1 - 1 \ \& \ X_2' \geqslant Y_2)$$

serve as X_1', X_2'. Now consider a cone $(\bar{X}_1 - 2^=, 0^{\geqslant})$, and try to expand list (6.4) by a state $\bar{X}_1 - 2$, Z_2. If the attempt succeeds, we would again expand our understanding of the state $\bar{X}_1 - 2$, Z_2, etc. If it is impossible to expand the list at the price of decreasing the first coordinate, take the cone $(0^{\geqslant}, \bar{X}_2 - 1)$, $(0^{\geqslant}, \bar{X}_2 - 2)$ .... . The process of extension of list (6.4) should terminate (a more general statement is proved in section 6.2). It ends either by crossing over boundaries on "both sides," that is, by generating states $(0, u_2)$ and $(v_1, 0)$, or even earlier—because of the inability to move to (t_1, t_2) from the corresponding cone. (By the way, in all these cases a cone is reduced to a ray.)

After the list is completed and the set of states X_1', X_2' is built, it is easy to check if this set can be reached from the initial state. Namely, if the initial state is located "below" (accordingly, to the left) of the terminating cone, then the set X_1', X_2' is unreachable. If the termination is caused by reaching the edge of the cone, then the set of states not belonging to X_1', X_2' is finite (that is, if X_1', X_2' is unreachable, then all trajectories coming from the initial state will terminate or go into a loop). On the other hand, if X_1', X_2' is reached, then its construction guarantees that we will be able to move to a state that is not less than X_1', X_2'.

The decidability of the most important property of TP-systems (for interpretation purposes)—the ability to move to the state that is not worse than a given one—is combined with their universality property: the ability to generate arbitrary r.e. sets. In particular, the following theorem holds.

THEOREM 2 It is possible to construct an undecidable two-resource TP-system defined by production functions, all of which, except one, are linear.

(The only nonlinear function is also simple. For example, it can be $2x - 1/x + 1/2$.)

A further decrease in the number of nonlinear functions leads to decidable systems. The case when all production functions are linear is the simplest and probably the most important one.

Definition A TP-system is called linear if

$$\forall \alpha; \ \beta; \ X, Y, Z \ ((\alpha, X) \vdash (\beta, Y) \ \& \ Z \geqslant 0 \Rightarrow (\alpha, X + Z) \vdash (\beta, Y + Z)). \quad (6.5)$$

We define TP by a finite list of the results of the work on some finite set of states (which can be expanded to other states by rule (6.5)). It corresponds exactly to the specification of rules of k-local calculi (with $k = n$). More precisely, if we take into account the difference between modes and resources, then the rules will have the form

$$\frac{|^{\langle\alpha\rangle}\square|^{\langle l_1\rangle}p_1\square\ldots\square|^{\langle l_n\rangle}p_n}{|^{\langle\beta\rangle}\square|^{\langle l_1'\rangle}p_1\square\ldots\square|^{\langle l_n'\rangle}p_n},$$

that is, the rules can be viewed as particular cases of $(*)$ from chapter 5, in which a variable p_0 is absent, leading to nonmonotonicity with respect to the right component of the state.

THEOREM 3   Any linear calculus is decidable.

Notice that the time complexity of the corresponding algorithm for the fixed calculus is not high: It can be limited by a polynomial of the parameters of the state. Theorems 1 through 3 together with the theorems on decidability from chapter 2 support our conclusion that all instructions violating the monotonicity condition for economic systems should be eliminated. (Recall that it can only improve the quality of the system.) Theorem 3 can be modified to show that even systems with nonmonotonicity with respect to exactly one recource are decidable. This can be interpreted as the possibility of preserving the predictability of the system, if its control is preserved, as the last resource, with the loss of monotonicity. Then this violation should be allowed for only one fixed type of resource (which we call *initiative*). When this resource is exhausted, the steps prescribed to the system are different from those available in the usual state; sometimes this can be convenient.

6.2   The Problem of Infinite Functioning of a System

The real awareness of the fact that the earth's resources are not far from exhaustion and that modern economy may irreversibly destroy the environment makes the problems of global economic strategy extremely important and urgent. The main question related to this problem concerns the role played by technological and scientific progress. Is it really true that the increase of informational and material potential of humanity is a sufficient (or necessary) condition of its survival? Or, perhaps, on the contrary, the theory of progress brought us to a dead-end, and the only way out is to put an end to this progress? Concrete ecology problems require concrete computations, but the general qualitative results discussed in what follows can also be of some interest. In the discussion it is important to notice that negative results can be obtained even if we assume that the improvement of technology and the growth of information are unlimited.

First, I describe a notion of an economic system (ES) more powerful than the one formalized by TP-systems. An ES is a pair of algorithms $[A, B]$. A will still be called the algorithm of functioning of the system, and B will be called the algorithm for the computation of resources. I assume that all states of the system as well as its resources and generated products are enumerated. As was done before, I consider only discrete resources and products. The time is also discrete; the unstable character of the ES is manifested by the explicit dependence of the algorithm of functioning on time. Given an arbitrary pair i, t (where i is the number of a state of the system and t is time), algorithm A produces a finite list of numbers—codes of states in which the system can move at time $t + 1$. Such states depend on decisions made by the system at moment t. Let us assume that i can belong to $A(i, t)$ (that is, the status quo may be preserved). A sequence i_0, $i_1, \ldots$ of numbers is called a functioning of the system from the initial state number i_0 if

$$\forall t \ (i_{t+1} \in A(i_t, t)).$$

The algorithm B is used to determine the complete list of resources available to the system in a given state i_t. (In terms of chapter 5, $B(i_t)$ computes $LR_{S(t)}$.) More precisely, $B(i)$ is the finite list of numbers $N_1, \ldots, N_m$ ($m \geqslant 0$), where N_j denotes the number of units of resource j in the ES in state i. The number of types of resources and products of the system can be unlimited; it is assumed that all resources with numbers greater than m are not available to the system in state i; that is, $B(i)$ can be viewed as an infinite list $N_1, \ldots, N_m, 0, 0, \ldots$.

Given a description of an SES or of a TP-system, it is easy to build the corresponding algorithms A and B, that is, to turn them into an ES. (It is important to differentiate between A in the ES and A in the TP-system.) The stable character of SESs and TP-systems is expressed by the fact that the dependence of the corresponding A on time is fictitious.

Let us divide all resources of an ES into material and information resources. I assume that the information resources can be generated in our system from "nothing," that is, without exhausting other resources. Such an idealization, which allows the unlimited growth of information, will only strengthen our further results. On the other hand, I assume that some restrictions on the possible growth hold for the material resources of a given ES. Let M be a set of material resources and $B^M(i)$ be a projection of $B(i)$ to M; that is, all numbers from $B(i)$ that correspond to resources not belonging to M become zeros. We say that an ES satisfies the *law of nonincreasing resources* (LNR) if for any functioning of the system

$$\forall k, l \, (k < l \Rightarrow \neg (B^M(i_k) < B^M(i_l)), \tag{6.6}$$

which means that, if $B(i_l)$ has more material resource of some type than $B(i_k)$, then $B(i_l)$ necessarily has less of some other material resource. We say that an ES satisfies the *law of decreasing resources* (LDR) if, in addition, $B^M(i_k) > B^M(i_l)$ or $B^M(i_k) = B^M(i_{k+1}) = \ldots = B^M(i_l)$. The LNR is satisfied to within λ if

$$\forall k, l \, ((k < l \, \& \, \neg (B^M(i_l) < \lambda \cdot B^M(i_k))) \Rightarrow \neg (B^M(i_k) < B^M(i_l))),$$

that is, if whenever $B(i_l)$ has λ times more units of a resource than $B(i_k)$, $B(i_k)$ has a bigger supply of some other resource. The LNR is satisfied starting from some place if system (6.6) is satisfied for $B^M(i_k)$ and $B^M(i_l)$ such that the sum of units of the material resources for them is greater than some number L. The important difference between the LNR and the LDR is the fact that the LNR allows a sequence $B^M(i_0), B^M(i_1), \ldots$ of the form $(1, 2; 2, 1; 1, 2; 2, 1, \ldots)$ and the LDR forbids it. The statements discussed in what follows allow two interpretations: "absolute" and "relative." The absolute interpretation is purely theoretical. It considers the world economy as an ES, and as the initial restriction on resources, it uses the resources of the planet (or of the solar system). The relative interpretation allows us to consider a regional (or some other specific) ES, to divide material resources into renewable and nonrenewable, and to introduce real restrictions on the resources of the given ES. For such interpretations it is natural to assume that our ES satisfies the LNR; this assumption is satisfied starting from some place p with a certain degree of accuracy. (The upper limit of renewable resources should play the role of the place p.)

Now we state several simple mathematical results. The most important of them is formulated by the following well-known assertion, which I call the *termination lemma.*

LEMMA   Let

$$X^{(1)}, X^{(2)}, \ldots \qquad\qquad\qquad\qquad (6.7)$$

be a sequence of n-ary vectors, the coordinates of which are positive integers. If

$$\forall k, l \, (k < l \Rightarrow \neg(X^{(k)} \leqslant X^{(l)})),$$

then the sequence (6.7) is finite.

We can prove the termination lemma by induction on n. If $n = 1$, then the statement is obvious. We know that in sequence (6.7) $X^{(1)} > X^{(2)}$, $X^{(2)} > X^{(3)}$, and, because the $X^{(i)}$ are nonnegative integers, the sequence terminates. But even for $n = 2$ there are possible sequences of an unpredictable length, such as $(5, 5)$, $(4, 10^{10})$, $(10^{998}, 4)$, $(4, 10^{10} - 1)$, $\ldots$, $(3, 95^{96^{97}})$ $\ldots$. But all of them should also terminate. Suppose that this is not the case and that sequence (6.7) is infinite. According to the inductive hypothesis, all sequences for $n - 1$ dimensions are finite. If sequence (6.7) is infinite, then there are arbitrary large numbers for some coordinate. Let it be the first coordinate, and consider a subsequence

$$S_n = X^{(i_1)}, X^{(i_2)}, X^{(i_3)}, \ldots$$

of sequence (6.7) that is *not descending* with respect to the first coordinate, that is, $X_1^{(i_1)} \leqslant X_1^{(i_2)} \leqslant X_1^{(i_3)}, \ldots$. Because this coordinate can take arbitrarily large values, the subsequence can be infinite. On the other hand,

$$\forall k, l \, (k < l \Rightarrow \neg(X^{(i_k)} \leqslant X^{(i_l)})),$$

which means that

$$\neg((X_2^{(i_k)}, \ldots, X_v^{(i_k)}) \leqslant (X_2^{(i_l)}, \ldots, X_v^{(i_l)})).$$

The inequality cannot be violated because of the first coordinate. Hence the sequence obtained from the subsequence S_n by deleting all the values of the first coordinate is a sequence of type (6.7) for $n - 1$ dimensions. According to the inductive hypothesis this sequence is finite. The contradiction proves the lemma.

Some generalizations of the lemma, together with arguments similar to those used in its proof, lead to the following five statements (in what follows an ES is called a *proper economic system* if there is a K such that during its functioning $B^{(n)}(i_j)$ changes at least once every K steps):

1. If an ES satisfies the LNR starting from some place to within a certain accuracy, then the number of different $B^{(n)}(i_j)$ is finite for any functioning. If, in addition, the informational ability of ES is limited, then it has only a finite set of states.

2. If an ES is a proper economic system that satisfies the LDR, then it will stop for any functioning and for any initial state.

3. On the other hand, even if an ES has no informational resources and satisfies the LDR, functionings of the ES can be arbitrarily long.

Statements 1 through 3 hold if the number of different resources and products in the system is limited. Many elements in lists $B(i)$ are bounded. If this restriction does not hold, then:

4. There is a proper ES without informational resources that satisfies the LDR and generates infinitely many $B(i_j)$.

Still some analog of statement 2 holds.

5. We say that a group of resources is necessary for an ES if, for each i such that $B(i)$ contains no elements of this group, the process of functioning stops. If there is a finite necessary proper group that satisfies the LDR, then the ES will stop for any functioning and any initial state.

I now derive some qualitative conclusions of statements 1 through 4. If we stop our search for the new resources and concentrate all our efforts on the improvement of the technology, then the ES of humanity will inevitably stop—even if we assume that every person can handle an arbitrarily large amount of information. The same is true even if the lists of resources and products are allowed to expand (except when there is an infinite sequence of replacements). It is important to notice, though, that any limit on the lifetime of the system can be exceeded by the use of this strategy. The forms of possible outcomes are related to the exclusion of some material resources from the scope of the LDR (for example, assigning higher priorities to the development of programs such as the space- or sea-exploration program, to gradual essential changes in the lists of resources, as well as to moving in the direction of nonproper ESs. For relative interpretations such solutions are fairly realistic.

As we can see, the accumulation of information and the improvement of technology do not give us a chance of an infinite progressive development but allow us to go into an infinite loop. An ES moving in this circle preserves its material finiteness but allows a progressive development in the sphere of information. This can be viewed as a realistic analog of the movement toward a nonproper ES. (The informational resources and products have distinct, essential characteristics that are distributed with respect to the demands and produced according to our abilities: The more our spiritual demands exceed our material needs, the closer we move to "the kingdom of freedom," reducing "the kingdom of necessity" to the routine circle of material production.) Obviously, removing restrictions on production of some resources as well as developing new resources and products should help in the search for the optimal cycle.

So, a far-seeing, long-term economic policy should aim neither at the development of material needs nor at slowing the progress of technology. It should concentrate on elevating the spiritual and creative potentials of the society, first because this will help to develop primacy of the spiritual in the psychology of the people and, second, because only fundamental research and fundamental technological developments can provide for the material side of the real progress of humanity.

Problems

1. Write a formula expressing that a system satisfy the monotonicity condition for all resources except possibly the third.

2. Give an example of a k-local calculus (a) with monotonicity violated for the second resource, (b) with monotonicity violated for all resources, and (c) without violation of monotonicity.

6.3   The Strategy of Increasing the Freedom of Choice

It is important for the theory of economic systems to develop non-price-based criteria for evaluating activity. The partial ordering $\leqslant$ of a material criterion or of a Pareto optimization or of a somewhat imprecise ordering by "variety" can be viewed as examples of such criteria. Ordering by variety is understood as the variety of system's products and services as well as the freedom of making decisions. The apparatus developed in this chapter allows us to try the system of ideas and notions related to such "variety" criteria and to make some qualitative conclusions.

From now on, by a TP-system I mean a linear TP-system. (The results can be partially extended to other production functions.)

Consider $I_{\langle A,Q \rangle}(p)$ as a function of Q. I investigate the strategy of increasing the freedom of choice, that is, the strategy of the development of the system in the direction of the Q's that maximize $I_{\langle A,Q \rangle}(p)$. More pecisely, if p is fixed (the less p is, the "smarter" our strategy), then the strategy forces us to move from a state Q such that $A(Q) = Q_1, \ldots, Q_l$ to a state Q_j such that

$$\forall_j \, (I_{\langle A,Q_j \rangle}(p) \leqslant I_{\langle A,Q_i \rangle}(p)),$$

where $Q \in \{Q_1, \ldots, Q_l\}$. This means that the step from Q to Q_i can only decrease the freedom of the system; the strategy forbids inactivity in this unfavorable case. If more than one state with the maximum value of I can be chosen, the strategy allows us to move to any one of them. Notice that, if p is decreasing, then commands given by the strategy can change—and not necessarily in a monotonic way; that is, it is possible that for p_1 and p_3 we have Q_1 selected, but for p_3 the choice is Q_2 (here, $p_1 > p_2 > p_3 > 0$).

The direct interpretation of p for economic systems is rather artificial. It is, roughly, the probability for the decision to be the last one before inspection: $I_S(p)$ reflects the number of states in which the system can be found by the inspection. But the introduction of p gives a natural picture of the gradual decrease of the influence of a given decision on the remote future. To see why this is so, notice that, to compute the freedom of choice at a state Q_0, we multiply the freedom of the system in the states immediately derivable from Q_0 by q; the freedom in the states obtained from Q_0 in two steps is multiplied by q^2, etc. Hence all the q's are well correlated with the so-called discount factor $\Gamma = 1/(1 + q)$.

This strategy is advantageous for many types of real economic systems and is used broadly on intuitive and empirical bases. As an example we can mention the strategy of increasing the activity of chess pieces used by chess players as well as by chess-playing programs. This strategy can be viewed as a particular case of our orientation to the maximization of I. Much can be learned about the properties of this strategy for simple systems, in particular for linear TP-systems. Linearity immediately implies that

$$\forall Q_1 Q_2 p \, (Q_2 \geqslant Q_1 \Rightarrow I_{\langle A,Q_2 \rangle}(p) \geqslant I_{\langle A,Q_1 \rangle}(p)).$$

A structure of the set of states derivable in a linear TP-system is rather simple and allows us not only to construct a deciding algorithm (the existence of which is proven in theorem 3 from section 6.1) but also to prove the following theorems (notice that the computation time of B and C from these theorems is not large).

THEOREM 1   For any (A, Q_0) there is an algorithm $B(p, \varepsilon)$ (where $0 < p < 1$, $\varepsilon > 0$, and values of B are states) such that

1. $B(p, \varepsilon) \in \langle A, Q_0 \rangle$, that is, state $B(p, \varepsilon)$ is derivable in (A, Q_0);
2. $\forall Q \ (Q \in \langle A, Q_0 \rangle \Rightarrow I_{\langle A, Q \rangle}(p) \leqslant I_{\langle A, B(p, \varepsilon) \rangle}(p) + \varepsilon)$;
3. $\exists \bar{p} (\bar{p} > 0 \ \& \ \forall p_1 p_2 \varepsilon_1 \varepsilon_2 (\bar{p} \geqslant p_1 \geqslant p_2 \ \& \ \varepsilon_1 \geqslant \varepsilon_2 \Rightarrow B(p_2, \varepsilon_2) \in \langle A, B(p_1, \varepsilon_1) \rangle))$.

The last condition is called the *stability* of B. It means that, if we want to satisfy condition 2 more thoroughly (that is, with more foresight with respect to p and with better precision with respect to ε), then we should move to the state $B(p_2, \varepsilon_2)$, which can be reached from $B(p_1, \varepsilon_1)$ constructed by a cruder method. Overall, the theorem says that we can move to the region with "saturated" freedom of choice where information cannot be increased by more than ε.

THEOREM 2   For any infinite (that is, open) system (A, Q_0) there is a stable algorithm $C(p, \varepsilon)$ such that

$$\forall Q \ (I_{\langle A, Q \rangle}(p) \leqslant I_{\langle A, C(p, \varepsilon) \rangle}(p) + \varepsilon).$$

The theorem says that the "saturation" occurs not only in the set of all derivable states but also in the set of all states in which the maximum possible freedom depends not on the initial state Q_0 but on the characteristics of the algorithm of functioning A. The set of states derivable from $C(p, \varepsilon)$ may be much "bigger" than the corresponding set for $B(p, \varepsilon)$ even in the sense of the number of dimensions and certainly in the sense of its information measure. The motion of a system from a state α, X to the state $\alpha, X + Z$ ($Z > 0$) is called *crediting* of the system. Using one crediting, it is possible to move to the region of maximum variety (where states $C(p, \varepsilon)$ are located). Let us denote the least upper bound of this variety by $\bar{I}_A(p)$ and the dimensionality of the corresponding set of states by l_A. The obtained results allow a natural interpretation.

1. Tuning by variety is indeed possible: By trying to increase the freedom of choice, the system moves to the regions that are more and more advantageous according to the material criterion or the cost criterion. This conclusion holds only for monotonic systems and supports the statement made at the end of section 6.1 about the expediency of lifting all restrictions on monotonicity.

2. For this type of tuning, saturation is inevitable. (Saturation occurs when a system moves to the region $B(p, \varepsilon)$.) The moment when saturation

occurs can serve as a signal telling us that we should start the reconstruction of the system, giving it more complex problems to solve. Saturation can be related to the exhaustion of abilities of the algorithm A or to the exhaustion or resources; that is, before A is enriched by new technologies, the method of crediting can be used to move the system into the region $C(p, \varepsilon)$ and to get closer to the maximum variety $\bar{I}_A(p)$ for our A. Obviously, this corresponds to the way this method is used in practice. (If a certain TP brings the system to the region of negative resources, then we may give it up or use a credit.)

3. This terminology can be used to capture the difference between changes in the infrastructure of the functioning algorithm and changes that are related to investments. The difference between two types of changes lies in the fact that infrastructural changes influence only the volume of the things produced by the system; that is, the natural form of such changes can be described by the increase of the length of vectors in the TP. Such an increase may help the system to move into the region of higher variety and to speed up such a motion; however, the dimensionality of the set of states of the system cannot become greater than l_A, and hence the power of infrastructural changes is analogous to the power of long-term crediting. Under favorable circumstances, these changes can increase the variety and make it greater than $\bar{I}_A(p)$, but they cannot guarantee that l_A will be achieved. Fundamental changes in the power of a system can be achieved by changes in the dimensionality of the set of vectors—technological possibilities of the algorithm A. Such changes influence not only the size but also the structural side of production and can be called investment-related changes.

The increase in variety is closely related to increasing the ability to show initiative. The opposite trend in tuning a system turns the CC into a technological entity without initiative. Such a transformation deprives the CC of its economic character (see section 5.2) and makes it possible (at least in theory) to replace this CC by a machine. If automation is impossible, then the lack of initiative should be met with other sources of freedom (for example, salary raises increase the variety of buying). If no reasonable solutions are found, individuals lose the sense of meaning of their activity. A system that is tuned by increasing the freedom of choice is aimed at broadening the set of possible solutions or, in other words, to broadening initiative. Giving people some level of independence is almost the only way to make them interested in what they are doing.

In this respect it may be interesting to investigate the problem of coordinating the interests of a system with the interests of its CCs when variety is chosen as one of the major criteria. The following trivial example shows how a conflict of interest can arise. Let a CC contain a rule

$$CC^1 : \frac{Ma_1}{a_2},$$

where M is large. The rule says that one CC of our system (say, CC^1) can produce a_2. The system as a whole is interested in the production of a_1 needed to produce a_2 (if it is tuned by the variety principle). On the other hand, if separate CCs are also tuned according to this principle, then they are not necessarily interested in the increase of the production of a_1 (except, of course, CC^1). Moreover, it is possible that the system will not be able to realize its goal (to generate a_2); that is, the dependence of the system on separate CCs may preclude it from obtaining the maximum variety.

Let us consider ways to subordinate the CCs to the interests of the ES as a whole.

1. The variety of the whole system is considered heavily in the set of criteria of each CC. This method has an "ideological character." The interest in the space program shown by a great number of people can serve as an example of such an approach. The advantages of this approach are obvious—and under extreme circumstances it is used by all types of societies. The disadvantages of this method are also clear: It is difficult to maintain the approach for a long period of time, and the approach also leads to the weakening of the interest of separate CCs in their own variety.

2. Goods can be formally divided into two groups A and B, balancing the lack of variety in possible decisions by increasing the variety in consumption. This method is flexible and broadly used. Its main shortcoming is that it stimulates redundant consumption (compare section 6.2).

3. Variety can be increased for a given CC by allowing the CC to take part in controlling the system. This can easily be formalized in the same mathematical theory by introducing mechanisms such as voting (see section 5.2). This method combines advantages of the first two but has an important drawback: It decreases the responsibility for management and makes it "loose."

At the present time, the measure of variety in terms of freedom of choice is evaluated intuitively. Its direct computation based on the definitions given in the beginning of this section is rather difficult. But some indirect evaluations are possible, such as the growth of credit, the improvement in the standardization of the intermediate products, and the increase of circulating capital. For strained plans the nomenclature demands (if they are satisfied) show the high level of variety in a system. For less strained plans the variety is manifested mainly by the development of new models and the improvement in quality of the products.

The improvement of reliability of the system and its ability to adjust to changes are among the most important advantages of the variety criterion.

7 Development by Rules

This plan, this picture is predetermined and envisaged beforehand. The amazing mutual subordination which we see in actions of life do not result from an accidental combination of physical and chemical phenomena.
Claude Bernard

He has hid his tail between his legs as a part of a well-considered plan, my boy.
Evgeny Shvartz

The growth of a living organism, the gradual evolution of a technical system, or the emergence of new biological forms—in short, any type of development—has the following three components:

1. Heredity—predetermination of the development of a system by its prehistory.
2. The influence of the system's environment.
3. Pure creativity.

In somewhat high-flown language we can say that the first two components belong to the kingdom of necessity, whereas the third one belongs to the kingdom of freedom. These three components may, of course, have different weights in the process of development. The evolution of the solar system, for example, is most likely determined by "heredity," the growth of a tree by heredity and environment, and the process of writing a poem mostly on the creative will of the writer, which is almost unpredictable from the outside.

A categorical statement of H. Bergson refers to the third component of development: "We cannot even imagine how it is possible to consider mathematically such things as organic creativity or evolution which constitute life in the proper meaning of this word" [22]. On the other hand, there are viewpoints according to which evolution is completely predetermined by "the kingdom of necessity" (even by the environment alone). I will not philosophize on the subject; instead in this chapter I analyze just the first two components of system development. The corresponding restrictions are formulated in section 7.1, and readers will be able to decide for themselves what types of "evolution" satisfy these restrictions and to what degree. Some possibilities of mathematical investigation of "pure creativity" (Bergson's objections notwithstanding) are considered in the next chapter.

7.1   Principles of Modeling

Heredity and death sit at the table with us.
Boris Pasternak

An evolution process can be treated only in the framework discussed if it satisfies with sufficient precision several conditions. The first of these conditions is called the *finiteness hypothesis* (see section 2.1). I restate it here.

FINITENESS HYPOTHESIS   For any moment of time it is possible to describe the state of the system using a finite amount of information.

More precisely, I talk about states described by finite collections of words over a finite alphabet (possible repetitions of words are allowed.)

EXAMPLE 19   Consider the evolution of a given make of car. We can view a huge word that corresponds roughly to the list of parts of a given car as an adequate description of the system's state. In doing so, we abstract out such characteristics of the system as the number of cars of the given make and individual features of each car. It is exactly such individual features (scratches, dents, etc.) that are most difficult to describe in finite words. In this example the list of parts (the same for each car of the given make) is analogous to the genotype of an object, whereas each particular car also has a phenotype, that is, some collection of special features determined by the interaction of the genotype with the environment (the quality of maintenance, mileage, number of accidents, etc.).

EXAMPLE 20   The complete description of a population should include all phenotypes, the whereabouts of the individuals, the description of the environment, the locations of food and natural enemies, and who knows what else. But in reality the representation of a population by a collection of its genotypes (together with the genotype frequencies or even without such frequencies, if we are interested in the investigation of mutations of pure lines under laboratory conditions) can serve as an adequate simplification suitable for modeling evolutionary properties of a population.

These two examples demonstrate entirely different types of systems (in [23] they are termed "rigid" and "corpuscular" systems), and both satisfy the finiteness hypothesis. Notice that this hypothesis can also be used for the study of the evolution of phenotypes (if the language of phenotypes is sufficiently well developed).

ENUMERABILITY HYPOTHESIS   For each state of the system, the set of states to which the system can move at a given moment of time is r.e.

When a state of the system is defined by one word, the hypothesis requires that the system be defined by its algorithm of functioning, which gives the set of immediate followers for each state of the system. Such sets can be infinite (see section 5.3). But even more important for our future discussion is the case of the "corpuscular" description of a developing system when the states are represented by finite collections of words.

An example of a system having a corpuscular description is the following. Let A be an alphabet. Words over A are interpreted as "corpuscles" (individuals or genotypes) of the developing system. Let L be an r.e. set of rules, that is, words of the form

$$S_1 \square S_2 \ldots \square S_m \vdash S_0 \qquad (m \geqslant 0), \tag{7.1}$$

where $S_0, \ldots, S_m$ are words in A and $\square$ and $\vdash$ do not belong to A. Rule (7.1) is interpreted as a possibility for "parents" $S_1, \ldots, S_m$ to have an "immediate descendant" S_0. Assume that L consists of a finite number of axioms $\vdash J_1, \ldots, \vdash J_k$. It is easy to prove that L defines an enumerable set M_l of all possible descendants of $J_1, \ldots, J_k$. We say that L defines a development system S_L if S_L is a deductive system that generates a finite collection of words in M_L, with the axiom $\{ J_1, \ldots, J_k \}$ and whose inference rules are:

1. The rule of dying, which allows the elimination of an arbitrary element.
2. The rule of birth, that is, the rule

$$\frac{\{R_1, \ldots, R_l\}}{\{R_1, \ldots, R_l, R_{l+1}, \ldots, R_{l+n}\}},$$

where there are $R_{i_1}, \ldots, R_{i_m}$ $(1 \leqslant i_j \leqslant l)$ such that L contains all words of the form $R_{i_1} \square \ldots \square R_{i_m} \vdash R_{l+j}$ $(1 \leqslant j \leqslant n)$.

It is easy to see that each finite subset of M_L is derivable in S_L. For a development system S_L the enumerability hypothesis means exactly the recursive enumerability of L.

To simplify the discussion, let us restrict ourselves to development systems that generate sets of words, that is, collections without repetitions. On the one hand this restriction is purely technical. But on the other hand it reflects the most interesting aspect of evolution proper: evolution for which essential steps are related to the creation of objects that differ from all previously created things.

EXAMPLE 19 (revisited)   Let me digress and discuss the evolution of the
means of transportation.

The basis consists of identical or similar "elementary ideas" inherent in the same
form to all nations. They are determined by inner reasons and follow from the
identical psychological organization of the mankind. The main types of tools or
weapons are the same for all people.... Like organisms these elementary ideas are
developing under the influence of the environment.
L. S. Berg

The history of inventions gives instructive examples of various combina-
tions of ideas that give life to new inventions. The mechanical combination
of the idea of rocking a log (that is, the idea of a road roller) with the idea
of portage gives a primitive tool for moving heavy loads. This observation
led to the discovery of the different functions of a road roller: the ability to
roll and the ability to carry a weight. Both abilities led to the road roller's
double role as the ancestor of both the wheel and the axis. The transformation of the road roller into the wheel and the axis turns portage on rollers
into the carriage. The further realization of the idea of a roller as the inter-
mediary between unmovable (road) and mobile (carriage) leads to the idea
of a bearing (as a boundary between the moving wheel and the motionless
axis). Understanding that the idea of a carriage contains an independent
idea of an engine leads to different forms of carts and wagons, with different
tractions, and later to the combination with the idea of a mechanical engine
(that is, to locomotives and cars), etc. This sort of description of evolution
of inventions can be done (at least in principle) rather formally by singling
out the finite number of elementary ideas and specifying a sufficiently broad
set of combination rules. It allows us (especially a posteriori) to describe
this evolution in the framework of corpuscular development systems (without repetitions). It can also help us to discover possibilities missed by
evolution and even to predict some new inventions.

Many results of this chapter (in particular, those about the relationship
between internal and external factors of development) are applicable to the
corresponding deductive system.

    The last hypothesis that is important for our approach is called the
Markovian hypothesis.

MARKOVIAN HYPOTHESIS   The process of development of the system can be
viewed as a Markov process with discrete time.

In other words, for each state of a given development system and each moment of time, we are given probabilities of application for each rule of birth and dying.

All three hypotheses form a basis of any application of the deductive systems apparatus in the spirit of "horizontal modeling." I believe that they are satisfied with reasonable accuracy by the majority of evolutionary (and even more general) processes that can be found in natural science. I certainly do not mean that the corresponding systems can actually be constructed or their probabilities computed. But it does not prevent us from understanding the qualitative picture.

Other hypotheses that I discuss are purely technical and introduced for simplicity. In particular, I use the following.

SIMPLIFIED MARKOVIAN HYPOTHESIS   States of the system are sets without repetitions.

It is known that the "gluing together" of states of a Markov chain can lead to the violation of its Markovian property. The set without repetitions can be viewed as the result of such an operation applied to an infinite number of states of a system with repetitions. Hence the simplified Markovian hypothesis is much more problematic and can be satisfied only approximately. Some arguments in its defense can be obtained from the existence of a fundamental difference between the duration of an evolutionary step and the duration of an individual's life. The problem of adequacy of this hypothesis is similar to the problem of moving to the macroscopic time scale in statistical physics.

7.2   The Extinction Theorem

Necrophile:
No, we can not select,
Nature selects,
He will die out
Who has come to the world to die out.
Olgas Suleymenov

Let L and M_L be as in section 7.1. By the simplified Markovian hypothesis there is an algorithm $A(x, t)$ that produces probabilities of possible moves at a given discrete moment t. The following moves from $X = \{p_1, \ldots, p_n\}$ are possible:

1. to $\{p_1, \ldots, p_{i-1}, p_{i+1}, \ldots, p_n\}$ (such a move is called reduction),
2. to X,
3. to $\{p_1, \ldots, p_n, Q\}$, where Q is a new word derivable from X in one step by a rule from L.

Let us assume that the probability of any reduction move is not equal to 0. Denote the sum of all such probabilities by $K(x, t)$ and the ratio of the largest probability to the smallest one by $M(x, t)$. Let us also assume that there are ε_0 ($\varepsilon_0 > 0$) and M_0 such that

$$\forall x, t \ (k(x, t) \geqslant \varepsilon_0 \ \& \ M(x, t) \leqslant M_0).$$

The interpretation of the second condition in terms of biological evolution looks like this: For any two species that come into existence in the process of evolution and reside on earth at the same period of time, one cannot be infinitely more viable than the other.

Under these conditions we can easily prove the following lemma.

LEMMA   For any two states X_1 and X_2 there is a state X_3 such that the process goes from X_1 to X_3 with probability 1 and $X_2 \cap X_3 = \varnothing$.

In other words, from any current state X_1 we necessarily move into a state that does not contain elements from a predefined set X_2 (in particular, all elements of X_1 will die out; to see this, just take X_2 containing X_1).

Let us also assume that S_L satisfies the condition of finiteness of potential prehistory: For any P in M_L there is a finite number of words from which P can by obtained by rules (7.1) of system S_L. For biological evolution, for example, the condition means that each species can be a descendant of only a finite set of other species (according to the traditional viewpoint, there is only one way by which species could have originated).

Under the conditions stated, we can prove the following theorem.

EXTINCTION THEOREM   For any state X and any word P there is a class of states that does not contain P and such that the process will go from X to a state from this class with probability 1.

EXAMPLE 5 (revisited)   For every word w over the alphabet $\{a, b\}$, the conditional viability $V(w)$ is defined by the following rules:

a. $V([ab]^{\langle n \rangle}) = \max\{101 - n, 1\}$ $(n = 1, 2, 3, \ldots)$;
b. $V(p) = 1$ if the number of occurrences of a in p is equal to the number of occurrences of b minus one;
c. otherwise $V(p) = 0$.

Consider $X = \{p_1, \ldots, p_n\}$. We assume that the total probability of reducing moves $K(x, t)$ is equal to $\frac{1}{4}$ for all x and t and is distributed among elements of X inversely proportional to their viability. The total probability of "increasing rules" is $\frac{3}{4}$ and is distributed in the following way: Rule a is applied to each p_i with the probability $3/(8n)$. Rule b or rule c is also applied with the same probability if it does not lead to zero viability; different applications of rule b appear with equal probabilities. If an application of a rule generates a word from X or a word with zero probability, then the next state is still X. Hence from $\{ababab, abbab\}$ we move to $\{ababab\}$ with probability $98/(4 \times 99)$ and to $\{abbab\}$ with probability $1/4 \times 99$. (We take into account that $V(ababab) = 98$ and $V(abbab) = 1$.) The probabilities of moving to $\{[ab]^{\langle 3 \rangle}, abbab, abab\}$ and $\{[ab]^{\langle 3 \rangle}, [ab]^{\langle 6 \rangle}, abbab\}$ are equal to $3/16$. (We have to take into account that there are two equiprobable applications of rule b to $[ab]^{\langle 3 \rangle}$, one of which generates a repetition.) The probability of saving a state unchanged can be computed as the sum of the probability of repetition $\{abbab\}$ and the probability of generating unviable $\{abbab\}^{\langle 2 \rangle}$ $(3/32 + 3/16 = 9/32)$.

For the assignment of probabilities described, the qualitative picture of evolution will look like this: States generated in the beginning will contain few words with low viability (that is, words containing $\{bb\}$). Almost identical viability of the words of the type $[ab]^{\langle n \rangle}$ for small n will cause the word ab to disappear with a probability close to 1 and make its reoccurrence highly unlikely (such a reoccurrence would require the existence of words with low viability). The same is true for all words of type $[ab]^{\langle n \rangle}$ with small n. Hence there is a high probability for a system to move into states that consist primarily of words with low viability. The reoccurrence of viable words under these circumstances is highly unlikely. Therefore we observe a shift toward states that consist of words with long derivations. This shift occurs despite the decreasing average viability of these words and the violation of the finiteness of prehistory condition. It can be seen that the extinction theorem is not applicable in this situation, because the word of the form $[ab]^{\langle n \rangle}$ stops dying irreversibly for n close to 100. Hence this example also demonstrates that the extinction theorem can be expanded to the following situations: (1) Only some derivable words have finite prehistory; (2) the potential prehistory of a given group of words is infinite but "blocked" by the much lower viability of some of their immediate predecessors (this is exactly what happens in our example).

7.3   From Inside or from Outside?

Environment only invites the organism to grow. Its function consists in exhibiting certain benevolence, which is gradually and continuously neutralized by its stern-ness which binds the living body and brings death to it.
Osip Mandelstam

The following question can be asked about any development system: To what degree is the development of the system determined by inner factors, and to what degree is it a consequence of external conditions? The history of science gives us many examples of intense and heated discussions on this subject. If we agree on leaving alone the third component of evolution (the presence of "pure creativity" is sometimes doubtful and sometimes touches on too deep a question of ontology), then the problem of relations between internal and external factors in the system's development can be formulated in sufficiently rigorous terms. If a development system is fixed and if the probabilities of its transitions are known, then the problem consists in defining the relationship between the evolution of the systems and varia-tions of probabilities.

First, it is important to realize that development systems tend to drift in the direction of states that consist of words with longer than average derivation (this is true for words that violate the finiteness of prehistory condition—their reappearance depends on the existence of increasingly long derivations). Some restrictions on this "law of development" are related to the possible existence of words violating the finite viability condition (which makes it possible for us to model "living fossils" and have optimistic views on the future of *Homo sapiens*). Hence if we witness a characteristic of an evolving system that can be interpreted in terms of improving its ability of adaptation, then we can conclude that this property is predetermined to a large extent by the deductive system and did not evolve "by itself" in the process of natural selection. (Recall that in example 5 natural selection results in the lowering of the average viability.)

Second, the degree of dependence of the products of evolution on the probabilities of individual moves is determined to a large extent by infor-mational characteristics of the initial deductive system. For deterministic systems, for example, the "play of probabilities" can lead to "abortion"— the unplanned end of development—but not to the change in the final product of evolution. More precisely, the degree of dependence is determined by the relationship between the deductive information (see section 7.4) and the average number of paths leading to the given state: If all paths lead to Rome, then probabilities assigned to individual paths on crossroads do not change the result. Hence the environment can affect only secondary characteristics of an organism, and an apple tree does not grow pears. On the other hand, a river that "can flow anywhere" but cannot return to the state it just left is determined completely by its environment, that is, by the relief of the surrounding country. The behavior and the location of a lone wolf depends strongly on the particular situation, whereas the same wolf bringing up pups is to a large extent predictable, even without information about its surroundings.

Therefore the degree of dependence is determined by the relationship between the deductive information in the development system and in its inversion (obtained by exchanging assumptions and conclusions in the rules of dying and birth). It is natural to name this relationship a measure of convergence. The fact that the history of the development of evolution theories is full of struggle between advocates of the convergence theory and its opponents is no accident. (The advocates of this theory stress the importance of convergence of traits of species separated by evolution and sometimes even not related to each other, whereas opponents of the convergence theory believe that such common characteristics are not very deep and can be explained completely by the similarity of the environment.)

It is worth noting that, even if the initial deductive system L is absolutely nonconvergent (each word derivable from M_L has a unique inference tree), the emerging development system S_L is inevitably convergent. (This is true for simplified systems without repetitions and even more so for systems whose states are defined as sets with repetitions.) Finally, we can state that the degree of dependence of evolution from its environment cannot be determined by general considerations but requires a special study of the measure of convergence of a particular calculus. Unfortunately, such calculi are not sufficiently well known.

The following question is important in this setting: What type of influence from the environment causes a development system to adapt to its environment? It is not difficult to see that the strong pressure of selection (that is, a large value of the coefficient $k(X, t)$) does not promote the increase of the average viability (even if such an increase is allowed by the initial deductive system). There is nothing paradoxical in this conclusion: It is well known that natural selection is often a conservative factor in evolution and stands in the way of new developments, especially if the advantages of such developments promise to show themselves only in the long run.

Undoubtedly, the tactic of balancing periods of "expansion" (when co-efficients of extinction are small, the environment is favorable, evolution occupies new ecological niches, etc.) and periods of "compression" (when natural selection claims control and revises the multiformity that emerged with its own knowledge) is wise. This assertion can be made more precise and can be proved formally. For a more detailed discussion, see [45, 50].

Problems

1. Show that every finite subset of M_L is derivable in S_L.

2. Prove the lemma and the extinction theorem.

3. State and prove the extinction theorem for the case when the finite viability condition and the finite potential prehistory condition are violated for some words.

4. Try to make the finite prehistory condition weaker.

5. Show that the probability that the word ab dies for the first time at a time not later than t tends to 1 when t grows.

6. For a development system, define a Markov chain in which k birth steps alternate with one dying step. Construct a system, in the spirit of example 5, so that the average viability decreases if three births alternate with two deaths and increases if thirty births alternate with twenty deaths.

III Vertical Modeling

Over abysses we stand,
Greedy and wretched, enchanted,
But the first solid staircases
Leading to cross-beams, to darkness,
Rise, as silent messengers,
Rise, as a mysterious sign!
There will be passages and rooms here,
There will be walls all over!
Oh, stubborn thoughts, remember!
You just forgot the draft!
It will come true, what you've designed,
The enormous building will rise to the heavens.
Valery Bryusov

8 To Fight and to Search: The Theory of Derivation Search

"Problem solving" is largely, perhaps entirely, a matter of appropriate selection.
W. Ross Ashby, *An Introduction to Cybernetics* (1958), p. 272

It is well known that the etymology of the Latin word "intellego" (inter + lego) is "choose among." This ancient meaning stresses the idea expressed in the epigraph to this chapter in a deliberately controversial form. I analyze the case when our creative task is to select not one action but a goal-directed chain of actions. Each of these actions transforms the problem into one or more related problems that I believe to be simpler than the initial problem.

8.1 Creative Activity as Derivation Search

I talk about the modeling of a creative process that results in a chain of arguments or actions chosen from some finite and well-defined set. The main problem in such a creative process is related to the necessity of intelligent organization of search, and not to selection and refinement of objects from completely undefined and unbounded sets, characteristic for another type of creativity.

The boundary between these two types of creative processes is relative for several reasons. First, when we talk about a creative process of the first type, it is not at all necessary to require the complete formalization of the corresponding sets. The important part is that the main problems in the process are related to sorting out different possibilities. Second, if it is necessary to make one selection from a not very well-defined fuzzy set, one can always try to analyze a sequence of actions that are used to build some kind of structure in this set. It is also worth noting that, even if a creative process of the first type is vigorously defined and all "moves" are completely formalized, we still have to analyze the absolutely informal creative process of a search for a desired chain of such moves.

In a real-life situation, the solution of crossword puzzles or playing cards requires creativity of the first type; however, solving a riddle involves the second type of creativity. For an artist, the second type of creativity is most likely predominant; however, for scientists, both types are mixed, even though the first often plays a more important role. The first type is also especially important for games with complete information and for theorem proving in a fixed and completely formalized theory.

The last problem gives us, most likely, the best model for the investigation of the first type of creative process. Indeed, in addition to the ability to check easily not only the correctness of each elementary logical inference but also the correctness of the derivation as a whole (such ability can be found in many other problems related to machine modeling of creativity, such as chess), the model has the following important property: All other creative problems of the first type can easily be reduced to it. The principles of such a reduction are well developed and clear to anyone who has studied mathematical logic (even though practical reductions of this sort are in many cases unreasonable and cause cumbersome and unnatural problems).

Hence mechanical theorem proving satisfies the universality criterion (see section 3.3). Ideas created in the process of solving such a problem must be of a rather general and universal character. Sometimes they are even too general.

The theory of mechanical theorem proving uses as its basis the part of mathematical logic that investigates how to find possible logical derivations of a given hypothesis or, in more general terms, how, given a deductive system and an object in its language, to find properties of the set of possible derivations of the object in the system. We are primarily interested in narrowing the class of possible derivations, in the discovery of deductive means sufficient for the verification of a given hypothesis, etc.

Remark   It was noted repeatedly that in some sense logic models human reasoning. (For example, the title of Boole's classical work is *An Investigation of the Laws of Thought*, and he states his goal as collecting "some probable intimations concerning the nature and constitution of the human mind.") But there is no doubt that logical apparatus models only the way we record the final products of our reasoning. It allows us to learn not how the brain discovers the truth but what it accepts as the truth. On the other hand, the main concern of the theory of derivation search is how the truth can be discovered.

Consider a class K of creative problems (in the defined sense). Based on specific characteristics of this class, select a deductive system $\mathscr{P}_K$ such that its axioms are problems for which solutions are known and whose inference rules $S_1, \ldots, S_m \vdash S_0$ guarantee the solvability of problem S_0 if the solutions of problems $S_1, \ldots, S_m$ are known. A given problem from K has a solution if it is derivable in $\mathscr{P}_K$. Finding a solution of a problem means finding one of its possible derivations in $\mathscr{P}_K$; finding an efficient solution means finding a short derivation.

Under favorable conditions $\mathscr{P}_K$ can be complete: A problem from K will have a solution if and only if it is derivable in $\mathscr{P}_K$. It is not difficult to achieve completeness for the type of creativity in which, for each situation, a set of all possible elementary moves is known. In this discussion I almost exclusively consider complete systems.

EXAMPLE 21   The problem of proving a theorem in a given theory can be used as a natural model of this situation. Axioms of the theory and its inference rules form $\mathscr{P}_K$. Proving a theorem means by definition finding its formal derivation in the theory. Different kinds of logic can be used for refining the notion of formal derivation and, if the logic is fixed, there are still many different deductive systems that can be used to formalize this logic. One of the most important logics and its formalization is completely described in section 8.2.

EXAMPLE 22. THE GAME OF CHESS   Consider the case of White playing to win. The problems to solve correspond to the positions in which White should make a move. Axioms of $\mathscr{P}_K$ are the positions where Black's king is in jeopardy. (We could select as axioms some other positions known to be winning. If White's goal were to make the game end in a draw, a different set of axioms would be selected.) Rule 1 of deductive system $\mathscr{P}_K$ can be constructed as follows: Given a position S_0, White's move M, and a set of all possible positions $S_1, \ldots, S_m$, which can be achieved by Black's responses to M, add the rule $S_1, \ldots, S_m \vdash S_0$ to $\mathscr{P}_K$. (The number of rules with the conclusion S_0, is equal to the number of all possible moves that White has in this position and, for every such rule, the number of premises is equal to the number of all possible responses of Black to the corresponding White move.)

These examples clearly show the difference between the formal character of a result and the informality of its discovery. We are interested in the analysis of this informal process and do not propose to construct, for instance, a chess program on the basis of writing out $\mathscr{P}_K$. Hence the complexity of $\mathscr{P}_K$ is not essential for our discussion. (As a last resort, we can write each rule 1 in the computer's memory at the moment when it is needed). Instead, we are going to concentrate on the question, What are the principal changes in our basic deductive systems whose discovery constitutes the essence of the creative process? What changes will take us to the next floor of our tower of deductive systems? Without such changes theorem-proving methods are practically useless in all cases except for the most trivial. In this respect the problem of derivation search from example 21, which seems natural and practically feasible, is not better than the cumbersome and relatively unnatural description from example 22.

EXAMPLE 23. THE CALCULUS OF INDEFINITE INTEGRALS   The tabulated integrals can be viewed as axioms of the calculus of indefinite integrals. The inference rules correspond to integration by substitution and by parts (and also to the standard transformations of elementary functions, such as factoring and integration of sums).

EXAMPLE 24. THE CALCULUS OF GEOMETRIC CONSTRUCTIONS   A problem to be solved is determined by an arbitrary collection of initial elements located in a plane. The axiom from which our construction should be derived consists in the diagram usually called "problem analysis" in high school geometry. The rules of inference correspond to drawing lines and circles, including the constructions of the required intersection points. (Notice that in the calculus of geometric constructions the transitions from premises to conclusions are accomplished by erasing a line and a circle. Another formalization of the same problem—more natural but less convenient for further use—can be obtained by making the construction of a "problem analysis" the goal.)

Example 24 shows that, even inside mathematics, the class of deductive systems used is much broader than the class of traditional "theorem-proving systems" with logicomathematical formulas as derivable objects. Moreover, having considered these examples, the reader may agree that the formalization of creative problems in logicomathematical terms most frequently is inadequate, even though from the theoretical standpoint it is equivalent to other formalizations.

This observation has already been made in relation to the universality criterion. Thus we need a theory of theorem proving in deductive systems of general type. On the other hand, it should not come as a surprise that such a theory will be similar in many respects to the theory of theorem proving in traditional logicomathematical systems [25].

We have seen (section 2.1 of chapter 2) that derivation-search algorithms can be constructed even for complex deductive systems. In other words, in principle we can solve every problem from K that has a solution. The practical significance of the theory of derivation search and its importance for modeling creative processes and for artificial intelligence is determined by the possibility of the gradual improvement of such algorithms.

What can be said on the basis of this discussion about the frequently repeated question, Can a machine think? One of the lame arguments often used by those who give the negative answer to this question is based on the assumption that all creativity related to selection is not creativity at all. The argument is not valid because it cuts off from modeling such high-level intellectual activities as mathematics and chess playing. If you have ever lost a game of chess to a machine (and most people on earth play chess significantly worse than modern chess-playing programs), then do not pretend that, when you play chess, it always seems to you that you are not thinking. Besides, try to prove that the creativity related to selection cannot be used to solve all possible problems (or at least that human intellect uses an entirely different approach).

So, instead of defending this unfortunate argument, let us think instead of a way that a machine can search for a proof in $\mathscr{P}_K$. Assume that problems from K really deserve the name "creative problems"; in other words, assume a problem with no trivial solutions, and assume that $\mathscr{P}_K$ contains common knowledge about these problems ("game rules" of examples 21 and 22). Then, most likely, the machine will be able to solve only the easiest problems of this class. What do experts in artificial intelligence do in this situation?

By considering theoretically and by pondering the experience of the masters in this field, the experts find the version of $\mathscr{P}_K$ that is much better suited for the derivation search than the initial one. In other words, they pull themselves and their machine to the next level of the tower of deductive systems. At this point the computer will win over people with restricted experience in the area. It will continue doing so until humans, with their ability to modify their own deductive systems, move to the next level. After that we will have the right to refuse to admit that a machine has the ability to think, even though it can "think" better than the average person. Modern machines exceed by far human abilities to do a mechanized search; however, humans tend to give the name "creative" only to the ability to improve one's derivation systems. At least for now. At present, machine modeling of this ability is just beginning to take shape. I hope that in the future mankind will teach machines to model or to simulate this ability; I hope even then we will have many reasons for self-respect.

EXAMPLE 21 (continued)   In the last decades there has been extensive discussion in the literature of the "superproblem" of modeling the process of proving new and difficult mathematical theorems on a computer. It is important not to confuse this "superproblem" with the use of machines in proving particular mathematical theorems (in previous years a proof of the four color problem by means of a computer made a great impression on the mathematical community). The main problem here is related to the fact that the psychological character of modeling mathematical thinking requires certain universality of the corresponding programs. The following aspects of the "superproblem" are of interest to us:

1. Delineating the boundaries of what can be achieved by modeling psychological activity on the machines based on the principles known today.
2. Developing new methods of interface between a human and a machine based on better knowledge of the "noncreative" parts of thinking.
3. Developing experimental techniques of comparison of different search methods that, at present, cannot be compared theoretically.

Experimental results can be summarized as follows: Even the best programs cannot handle theorems that are of interest to experts; but they can successfully compete, say, with gifted high school students who have never studied group theory and have just learned the axioms of a group. I believe this result should be viewed at this time as neither encouraging nor disappointing.

Problems

1.   Describe the 15-puzzle as a calculus $\mathscr{P}_K$.

2.   Discuss the contents of this section on the example of any game whose complete theory is known to you. For this game write a program that wins in every winning position.

8.2   Bottom-Up Search

"My friend, if you knew all about Cathy—her habits, friends, desires, dislikes, hopes, fears, dreams, intentions, and the like—do you think you would be able to find her?"
   "I'm sure I could," Marvin said.
   "Even without knowing the Theory of Searches?"
   "Yes."

"Well then," Valdez said, "apply that same reasoning to the reverse condition. I know all there is to know about the Theory of Searches, and therefore I need to know nothing about Cathy."
R. Sheckly

In this section and the next I discuss some of the ideas developed through the theory of logical deduction and their extensions to nonlogical deductive systems. In section 8.4 a more systematic and theoretical treatment of examples of improving deductive systems is given.

Gentzen's Calculus

Let us consider a deductive system C, known as the sequent or Gentzen variant of classical predicate calculus. The alphabet of C consists of the symbols $\sim$, $\wedge$, $\exists$, $\forall$, $\Rightarrow$, $($, $)$ of three infinite lists, called the lists of object, function, and predicate variables. The infinity of the alphabet and the meaning of logical symbols should be understood as in example 3 of chapter 1. Each predicate and function variable is assigned a positive integer, called the *arity* of this variable. The terms are object variables, function variables of arity 0 (that is, function constants), and expressions of the form $f(t_1,\ldots,t_k)$, where $t_1,\ldots,t_k$ are terms and f is a function variable of arity k. The terms that do not contain occurrences of object variables are called *ground terms*. An expression $P(t_1,\ldots,t_n)$, where $t_1,\ldots,t_n$ are terms and P is a predicate variable of arity n, is called an *atomic formula*. Now we can give the definition of a "formula."

1. Every atomic formula is a formula.
2. If F_1 and F_2 are formulas, then $\neg F_1, (F_1 \wedge F_2), (F_1 \vee F_2)$ are formulas.
3. If x is an object variable and if F is a formula that does not contain occurrences of $\forall x$ and $\exists x$, then $\forall x F$ and $\exists x F$ are formulas. All occurrences of x in $\forall x F$ and $\exists x F$ are called bound.

Let Γ_i be a (possibly empty) list of formulas. An expression of the form $\Gamma_i \Rightarrow \Gamma_2$ such that all occurrences of variables in it are bound is called a *sequent*.

Axioms of C are sequents of the form $\Gamma_1 F \Gamma_2 \Rightarrow \Gamma_3 F \Gamma_4$, where F is an arbitrary formula. Inference rules of C can be divided into six groups (each rule is followed by its symbolic designation):

a. $\dfrac{\Gamma_1 \Gamma_2 \Rightarrow F\Gamma_3}{\Gamma_1, \neg F, \Gamma_2 \Rightarrow \Gamma_3}$ $(\neg \Rightarrow)$ $\qquad$ $\dfrac{\Gamma_1 F \Rightarrow \Gamma_2 \Gamma_3}{\Gamma_1 \Rightarrow \Gamma_2, \neg F, \Gamma_3}$ $(\Rightarrow \neg)$.

b. $\dfrac{\Gamma_1, F_1, F_2, \Gamma_2 \Rightarrow \Gamma_3}{\Gamma_1, (F_1 \wedge F_2), \Gamma_2 \Rightarrow \Gamma_3}$ $(\wedge \Rightarrow)$

$\dfrac{\Gamma_1 \Rightarrow \Gamma_2, F_1, \Gamma_3; \Gamma_1 \Rightarrow \Gamma_2, F_2, \Gamma_3}{\Gamma_1 \Rightarrow \Gamma_2, (F_1 \wedge F_2), \Gamma_3}$ $(\Rightarrow \wedge).$

c. $\dfrac{\Gamma_1, F_1, \Gamma_2 \Rightarrow \Gamma_3; \Gamma_1, F_2, \Gamma_2 \Rightarrow \Gamma_3}{\Gamma_1, (F_1 \vee F_2), \Gamma_2 \Rightarrow \Gamma_3}$ $(\vee \Rightarrow)$

$\dfrac{\Gamma_1 \Rightarrow \Gamma_2, F_1, F_2, \Gamma_3}{\Gamma_1 \Rightarrow \Gamma_2, (F_1 \vee F_2), \Gamma_3}$ $(\Rightarrow \vee).$

d. $\dfrac{\Gamma_1, F(t/x), \forall xF, \Gamma_2 \Rightarrow \Gamma_3}{\Gamma_1, \forall xF, \Gamma_2 \Rightarrow \Gamma_3}$ $(\forall \Rightarrow)$

$\dfrac{\Gamma_1 \Rightarrow \Gamma_2, F(t/x), \exists xF, \Gamma_3}{\Gamma_1 \Rightarrow F_2, \exists xF, \Gamma_3}$ $(\Rightarrow \exists),$

where $F(t/x)$ is the result of simultaneous substitution of t for occurrences of object variable x and where t is a ground term.

e. $\dfrac{\Gamma_1, F(a/x), \Gamma_2 \Rightarrow \Gamma_3}{\Gamma_1, \exists xF, \Gamma_2 \Rightarrow \Gamma_3}$ $(\exists \Rightarrow)$ $\dfrac{\Gamma_1 \Rightarrow \Gamma_2, F(a/x), \Gamma_3}{\Gamma_1 \Rightarrow \Gamma_2, \forall xF, \Gamma_3}$ $(\Rightarrow \forall),$

where a is a function constant that does not occur in the denominators.

f. $\dfrac{\Gamma_1 \Rightarrow \Gamma_2, F, \Gamma_3; \Gamma_4, F, \Gamma_5 \Rightarrow \Gamma_6}{\Gamma_1, \Gamma_4, \Gamma_5 \Rightarrow \Gamma_2, \Gamma_3, \Gamma_6}$ (cut-rule).

Here and in what follows, the deductive system C is viewed as a purely formal syntactic object, independent of any interpretations of its symbols. The interpretation of C, however, could be easily understood by anyone familiar with the language of mathematical logic. There is one symbol that probably needs explanation. The sequent $A_1, \ldots, A_n \Rightarrow B_1, \ldots, B_n$ is interpreted as a metastatement: $A_1 \& \ldots \& A_n$ implies $B_1 \vee \cdots \vee B_n$. The reader may find it useful to relate this interpretation to example 3 and to arithmetical terms. It is important to realize, however, that this logical semantics is not at all necessary for understanding the problem of search for formal derivations in C.

EXAMPLE 21 (continued)   From the informal point of view, the main characteristic of C is its suitability for the formalization of logical rules for a broad set of mathematical problems. For example, consider the following statement: For any binary relation R and a function $f(y)$, if every pair $(x, f(x))$ satisfies R, then for any x there is a y such that (x, y) also satisfies R. This statement can easily be written in C as a sequent $\forall x R(x, f(x)) \Rightarrow \forall x \exists y R(x, y)$. The formal derivation of this sequent in C is

$$\frac{\dfrac{R(a, f(a)) \Rightarrow R(a, f(a))}{R(a, f(a)) \Rightarrow \exists y R(a, y)}}{\dfrac{\forall x R(x, f(x)) \Rightarrow \exists y R(a, y)}{\forall x R(x, f(x)) \Rightarrow \forall x \exists y R(x, y)}} \quad \begin{array}{l} (\Rightarrow \exists) \\ (\forall \Rightarrow). \\ (\forall \Rightarrow) \end{array}$$

Cut Elimination

In order to check the derivability of an object S in a deductive system $\mathscr{P}$, it is natural to use bottom-up derivation search. For each S its immediate predecessors can be obtained in one step by the application of one of the inference rules of $\mathscr{P}$. We can apply the same operation to such predecessors that are not axioms of $\mathscr{P}$ and continue the process for as long as possible. The tree constructed by such a process is called a derivation search tree; it becomes a derivation tree when all its leaves become axioms of C. Taking a close look at C from this perspective shows that all its rules except the cut rule are ideally suited for computing immediate predecessors of S.

A fundamental result by Gentzen guarantees that the set of objects derivable in C will not change if the cut rule is deleted from the list of inference rules of C. An inference rule is called admissible if its addition does not change the set of derivable objects. Gentzen's result shows that the cut rule is admissible in the calculus with the rules a through e.

Similar results about the specialization of a form of derivation were obtained by Herbrand several years before Gentzen's work was published. Herbrand's theorem (see [30]) can be conveniently stated for closed prenex formulas, that is, for formulas F of the form

$$\exists x_1 \forall y_1 \ldots \exists x_n \forall y_n M(x_1, y_1 \ldots x_n, y_n),$$

where M does not contain $\forall, \exists$. It can be shown that every predicate formula can be written in this form. Formula F is used to construct the so-called functional form of F:

$$F^\varphi = \exists x_1 \ldots x_n M(x_1, f(x_1), \ldots, x_n, f(x_1, \ldots, x_n)),$$

which can be obtained from F by deleting all universal quantifiers and replacing all y_i in M by $f(x_1, \ldots, x_i)$. $F_1, \ldots, F_n$ are new function variables of the corresponding arities. Herbrand's universe of F consists of all terms that can be constructed from the constants of F (or an arbitrary constant c if F does not contain constants) and function variables from F. Rewrite F as $\exists x N(x)$, where N does not contain quantifiers. A Herbrand disjunction of F by definition is an arbitrary formula of a form $N(t_1) \vee \cdots \vee N(t_k)$. Herbrand's theorem says that the derivability of F in C is equivalent to the derivability in the propositional calculus of one of Herbrand disjunctions of F. Sequent methods are applicable in a wider area than Herbrand's methods. It can be said that the methods of Herbrand and Gentzen represent a step in the development of the theory of logical deduction. At present, the cut rule is eliminated from the overwhelming majority of logical and logicomathematical calculi. Moreover, in most cases it is possible to construct a calculus that satisfies the following "subformula" property: A derivation tree of a formula F contains only subformulas of F. For second-order calculi and for arithmetic, the subformula property cannot be achieved, making the derivation search in such calculi extremely difficult. But even in these cases cut elimination allows us to obtain important information about the structure of derivations.

It is important to realize that, although cut-free derivations are easier to find, they can be much longer than derivations with cuts. It has been proved that derivations in propositional calculus can be shortened exponentially by adding the cut rule to the standard resolution rule.

For classical and intuitionistic predicate calculi (with or without equality), an increase in the length of derivations caused by cut elimination cannot be bounded by any "tower" of exponents. The corresponding comparison of proofs in Hilbert's calculus and a system with the resolution rule can be found in [26]; Hilbert's version contains the rule $A, A \rightarrow B \vdash B$, which is an analog of cut.

C-Rules

In general terms bottom-up search in a system is possible if it does not contain a rule such that for a fixed conclusion S_0 there can be an infinite set of corresponding lists of assumptions $S_1, \ldots, S_m$. Such rules are called *cut-type rules*, or *C-rules*. The problem of eliminating C-rules is important for a great number of calculi, not just logical ones.

In the system for indefinite integrals discussed, we can think of eliminating the general C-rule of integration by substitution, replacing it with permitting substitutions only of basic elementary functions. The general rule, then, can be modeled by composition of such restricted rules. (Binary addition and multiplication should be included in the set of elementary functions; it is natural to use differential forms for modeling the corresponding compositions.)

Another interesting example of a system that allows useful C-rule elimination is the calculus of geometric construction problems (see example 24). Instead of adding an infinite number of arbitrary lines and circles to the diagram, we can consider only those lines that pass through points already marked and those circles that have centers in such points and radii equal to distances between them.

It is worth noting that common logical systems contain C-rules even after cut elimination. Indeed, a set of possible terms used by rules ($\forall \Rightarrow$) and ($\Rightarrow \exists$) is infinite. The lack of knowledge as to how terms t should be selected constitutes the main problem for the efficient organization of bottom-up derivation search in such systems. We consider some ways to overcome these difficulties. Let us start with the most natural one.

Rules ($\forall \Rightarrow$) and ($\Rightarrow \exists$) are called *minus rules*, and the transformation of proofs that lead to the elimination of the infinity of choices in the selection of terms for these rules is called *minus normalization*. It was discovered that it is enough to consider instances of minus rules that contain only those terms that occur in the conclusion of these rules. (If the conclusion contains no terms, some special fixed constant is used that does not depend on instances of our rules.) It is possible to specify even more restrictive conditions on the domain of values of t used in minus rules. Moreover, it is possible to extend ideas of minus normalization to other logical systems.

C-rules are now eliminated from practically all important logical systems. The same idea can be used to eliminate C-rules from nonlogical systems. For example, the elimination of integration by substitution has exactly this character. Unfortunately, minus normalization in many cases does not produce the desired effect. Indeed, if the bottom-up application of a minus rule actually requires substitution of the term that does not occur freely in the conclusion of the rule, then our restriction only postpones the construction of the desired derivation. It prolongs our search and worsens the quality of its result. The lack of productiveness of such a restriction can also be demonstrated by the example with integration by substitution. Some estimates related to minus normalization can be found in [27]. One of the characteristic properties of all methods of C-rule elimination considered so far is the lengthening of the resulting derivation. At the same time, in all such methods, the new derivation is constructed in the initial language—an attractive property of these methods. It is also important to remember that such methods are not universal. It is possible to construct fairly simple deductive systems from which C-rules cannot be eliminated without changing the initial language of the system (see also [28]). But if we allow some well-interpreted change in the language and in the form of objects derivable in the initial system, we can eliminate C-rules from any deductive system without worsening the quality of the resulting derivation. Such a possibility was suggested by Kanger [29] (and also, independently, by Shanin and Pravitz) and was called the method of meta-variables.

Method of Metavariables

Initially, the method of metavariables was developed to eliminate the minus rules of deductive system C. The t used in these rules can be viewed as a metavariable that ranges over the set of all ground terms of the system C. This metavariable has the following important property, which is respon-sible for the existence of c-rules in C: t occurs only in the assumptions, not in the conclusions, of minus rules. F_i, Γ_i, a, and x can also be viewed as metavariables. What is special about t is that it occurs in the premise of the minus rule but not in its conclusion. (And this is the reason why we have a c-rule here; the metavariable a in rules $(\exists \Rightarrow)$ and $(\Rightarrow \forall)$ can be viewed as a metavariable whose domain consists of just one object, which shows that essentially no search is needed in counterapplications of these rules.) Metavariables that satisfy this property are called *proper variables* of the c-rule.

The method of metavariables is based on the explicit introduction of proper variables of minus rules into the language of our deductive system. The values of such variables are left unspecified in the bottom-up applica-tions of inference rules. In this way we gradually construct incomplete inference patterns. From time to time, we check whether it is possible to select values of the metavariables that will transform these patterns into a real derivation. This method for the C system in the form suggested by Prawitz can be found in [30, ch. 9]. Notice:

1. The set M^* of copies of disjuncts of M discussed in section 9.2 of [31] is our inference pattern.
2. The main substitution θ^* transforms this inference pattern into a real inference (more precisely, into a sequent $(M^*\theta^* \rightarrow)$ that can be derived in propositional logic).
3. The interpretation of variables from M^* as not bounded by universal quantifiers essentially introduces the new type of variables with the set of all ground terms as their domain.

The method of metavariables at first may seem to be a meaningless trick: Instead of selecting the necessary term when it is needed, we simply postpone the problem until later. But such postponing has an important advantage because we wait until the moment when all additional information necessary for making the decision is available. This allows us to change the direction of our search, and this change of direction turns out to be the most important idea used in modern proof-search methods.

In fact, the method of metavariables is a broadly used method of solving creative problems related to selection. It is often used inside mathematics. For example, the well-known method of "undetermined coefficients" can be viewed as a particular case of the method of metavariables. This role is especially clear in its application to the "calculus of antiderivatives." Moreover, important progress in mathematics has frequently been achieved by the introduction of metavariables in an old language. An especially clear example of such progress is given by transition from arithmetic to algebra, which consists entirely of expanding the language of mathematics by using expressions with variables and their transformation rules. In general, the functioning of a mathematical abstraction is closely related to its being the domain of metavariables in mathematical reasoning.

The use of metavariables is also characteristic for game poblems. Thinking about, say, a chess combination, we usually equate positions that could be obtained by "inessential" moves of our opponent. If one such move proves to be important for the development of the combination, we refine the domain of our metavariable and remove the corresponding position from the set of positions produced by "inessential" moves. Many important improvements of the selection mechanisms are related to the introduction of useful admissible rules (and sometimes of admissible axiom schemata). The calculus of antiderivatives, for example, can be expanded by the axiom scheme "An antiderivative of a rational function is elementary" or by admissible rules in the form of recurrent formulas. Other examples and some mathematical methods of comparison of selection improvements can be found in [32, 33].

8.3   The Idea of Metavariables in Local Derivation Procedures

The direct application of the method of metavariables to derivation search is rather difficult: The process of transformation of an incomplete inference pattern into a proof may require a huge amount of work; moreover, if such a transformation is impossible and if we have to expand the incomplete inference pattern to obtain the proof, then most of this work is useless. This happens mainly because our algorithm requires global knowledge of incomplete inference patterns. The correct selection of values of meta-variables is based on information about different parts of such patterns (a metavariable may occur in different branches of a derivation-search tree). This strongly suggests the necessity of combining the idea of metavariables with the idea of local derivation procedures.

The following fact is important for a better understanding of these statements: A derivation of a goal S in an arbitrary calculus $\mathscr{P}$ can be reduced to a derivation of a special object $\square$ in a special calculus $I_{\mathscr{P},S}$. Such an approach is common for modern derivation-search methods based on resolution: Disjuncts from S serve as axioms of $I_{\mathscr{P},S}$, and the resolution principle is used as the inference rule.

It is not difficult to describe bottom-up search in Gentzen-type calculi (for example in C) in similar terms. If Σ is an arbitrary sequent, then Σ is an axiom of $I_{C,\Sigma}$, and inference rules will transform objects $\Sigma_1*\ldots*\Sigma_i*\ldots*\Sigma_n$ into the following objects:

a. $\Sigma_1*\ldots*\Sigma_{i-1}*\Sigma_{i+1}*\ldots*\Sigma_n$ if Σ_i is an axiom of C.
b. $\Sigma_1*\ldots*\Sigma_{i-1}*\Sigma_i'*\Sigma_{i+1}*\ldots*\Sigma_n$ if Σ_i is obtained from Σ_i' by a one-premise rule.
c. $\Sigma_1*\ldots*\Sigma_{i-1}*\Sigma_i'*\Sigma_i''*\Sigma_{i+1}*\ldots*\Sigma_n$ if Σ_i is obtained from Σ_i', Σ_i'' by a two-premise rule.

A derivation of an empty object in $I_{\mathscr{P},S}$ corresponds to a generation of axioms on all branches of the corresponding derivation search tree in C.

Similar techniques can be applied to the method of metavariables. Let us extend our language by a potentially infinite alphabet and replace rule a by the global rule $\Sigma_1*\ldots*\Sigma_n/\square$ if there is a substitution of terms for metavariables that transfer Σ_i into tautology. The unnaturalness of this rule is obvious. Indeed, all other rules of $I_{\mathscr{P},S}$ are "local"; their application requires only partial information about the corresponding derivation-search tree (Gentzen's method requires the knowledge of Σ_i, and the resolution method requires the knowledge of two premises). This makes the complexity of their applications negligible with respect to the complexity of a derivation search. This is not the case for the global rule. The complexity of its application can be compared with the complexity of the corresponding derivation search. This observation justifies the division of derivation-search methods into local and global methods. (A method is global if it uses global rules and is local otherwise.) Notice that, for Prawitz's form of the method of metavariables, M is an axiom, rules of copying disjuncts from M are local rules, and the rule of transition from M^* to $\square$ (when M^* is inconsistent) is global.

At present the only methods that can be successively handled by computers are local methods. That is why the next step in the development of derivation-search methods was introducing local methods that use the main idea of the method of metavariables: Specify values of terms only when it is necessary. In the resolution method this idea is implemented by means of the notion of the most general unifier and is responsible for the fact that final values of terms became known only after $\square$ is derived. Two other methods—the clash method and the inverse method—can be viewed as local methods with metavariables. (Secondary methods obtained from these two by specifying the corresponding search strategies can serve as further examples.)

Digression. A Modification of the Resolution Calculus   The calculus

$$E = I_C, \{p(x, q, f(x)), \neg p(x, y, z) \vee \neg p(z, y, u) \vee p(x, f(y), u)\}$$

used for an efficient derivation search for "difficult" formulas from [26] can serve as a good illustration of the ideas from section 8.2.

Search for its admissible rules brings us to the rule

$$\{p\{x, y, T(x)\}\} \vdash \{p(x, f(y)), T(T(x))\}$$

for an arbitrary term T. This leads to the following metatheorem of E:

$$\forall mn \exists l (\vdash p(f_a^m, f_a^n, f_a^l)).$$

This metatheorem allows us to establish the derivability of the corresponding C_k in linear time (with respect to k). The practical method used to derive these formulas is close to the one described and differs significantly from the resolution method (as well as from the method of the British Museum).

The Inverse Method for C

I outline the inverse method for the simplest case when the goal of a derivation is a sequent $\rightarrow F$, where $F = \exists x_1, \ldots, x_n \, (\bigwedge_{i=1}^{k} D_i)$ and D_i are disjuncts. (Notice that the role of disjuncts in this standardization of formulas of C is complementary to the role played by disjuncts in the resolution method.) Expressions

$$[(i_1, Q_1); \ldots; (i_h, Q_h)], \tag{8.1}$$

where $1 \leqslant i_1, \ldots, i_h \leqslant \delta$ and $Q_1, \ldots, Q_h$ are substitutions of terms for $x_1, \ldots, x_n$, are called h-ary F-assemblages and are interpreted as the formula $D_{i_1}\theta_1 \vee \ldots \vee D_{i_h}\theta_h \vee F$. Calculus $I_{C,F}^\circ$, called the calculus of favorable assemblages, is defined by the following two rules:

RULE A   If $D_{i\eta}$ (or $D_{i\eta} \vee D_{i\xi}$) is a tautology, then $[(i, \eta)]$ (correspondingly $[(i, \eta); (i, \xi)]$) is a favorable F-assemblage.

RULE B   If F-assemblages $[H_1; (1, \xi_1)], \ldots, [H_\delta; (\delta, \xi_\delta)]$ are favorable, then an assemblage $[H_{1\eta_1}, \ldots, H_{\delta\eta_\delta}]$, where $\xi_1, \ldots, \xi_\delta, \eta_1, \ldots, \eta_\delta$ are substitutions such that $\xi_1\eta_1 = \ldots = \xi_\delta\eta_\delta$, is also favorable.

It is possible to show that the derivability of the 0-ary assemblage $\square$ in this calculus is equivalent to the derivability of F in C. (Moreover, minimal $\eta_1, \ldots, \eta_\delta$ can be selected at each step similar to the way it is done in the definition of the most general unifier.)

F-assemblages characterize the general type of formulas that could occur in a derivation tree of the sequent $\rightarrow F$. This allows us to reduce the potentially infinite set of subtrees of Gentzen's derivation-search tree to a finite set of F-assemblages (in particular, a finite number of initial favorable assemblages is sufficient to encode all nodes of all derivation trees of F in C (see rule A)). We can see that this method also combines the ideas of localization and metavariables.

I proposed the inverse method concurrently with Robinson's resolution method (see [33–38]). Initially the inverse method was intended for the calculus C. For the standardized formulas both methods are almost equally efficient. This statement can be confirmed by theoretical estimates (see [37]) as well as by a machine experiment [39]. It should be noted that standardizations that are best suited for the inverse method are exactly those that are the least suited for the resolution. A more important fact is that the inverse method is applicable to arbitrary sequents. (It is known that the standardization of formulas can significantly increase their length and create problems for the derivation search.) Moreover, this method can be extended to arbitrary sequent calculus without the cut rule. It can be said that the difference between the resolution and the inverse methods is similar to the difference between Herbrand's theorem for standard formulas and the whole complex of cut-elimination theorems.

General Schema of the Inverse Method

For any calculus K with the subformula property and any sequent E, let us build a derivation of E. In this process the structure of the uppermost sequents of the potential derivation tree is determined first; the structure of sequents located immediately under them is determined next, and so on. Hence this method is inverse with respect to bottom-up search. The goal is achieved by building a calculus $I_{\mathscr{P},\Sigma}^{\circ}$ of favorable assemblages. The objects derivable in this calculus are pairs $[L, B]$, where L is a list of subformulas of Σ and B is a system of relations between elements of L. (More precisely, L consists of codes of some subformulas of Σ chosen in advance.) For each sequent Σ_1 and each Σ-assemblage H, the relation "H belongs to Σ_1" is defined. Rules A and B are formulated for initial and generated favorable assemblages correspondingly. The following two conditions are required for the correctness of the method:

a. For any Σ-assemblage H generated by rule A and for any sequent Σ_1, if H belongs to Σ_1, then Σ_1 is derivable in K.
b. For any Σ-assemblage H generated from favorable arrays by rule B and for any sequent Σ_1, if H belongs to Σ_1, then Σ_1 is derivable from K.

If all notions are suitably defined, then the completeness of the method can also be guaranteed: Σ is derivable in K if and only if the empty Σ-assemblage is favorable. So, as we can see, for the definition of a particular inverse method the following should be specified:

1. An algorithm to code those subformulas of Σ that are necessary for the definition of the Σ-assemblage.
2. A language for the definition of the system of relations.
3. Rules A and B, satisfying conditions a and b.

To guarantee the metavariable property, we should make sure that the results of applications of rules A and B belong to as many sequents as possible.

Besides the orientation to practical derivation search, the inverse method has a number of qualities that make it a convenient theoretical tool for investigation of decidable classes of formulas and of reduction classes. It is used to obtain generalizations of known results, to discover new decidable classes and reduction classes, and to give a general schema uniting almost all known results on decidable classes of formulas of classical predicate calculus. To illustrate the use of the inverse method for such applications,

I prove the decidability of the class of formulas of the form

$$\exists x_1 \ldots x_n \forall y_1 \ldots y_l \, (D_1 \,\&\, D_2),$$

where D_1 and D_2 are disjuncts without functional symbols. (To make the discussion closer to the definitions for the inverse method, we can rewrite this formula as

$$F = \exists x_1 \ldots x_n \, (D_1(x_1, \ldots, x_n), f_1(x_1, \ldots, x_n), \ldots, f_1(x_1, \ldots, x_n))$$

$$\&\, D_2(x_1, \ldots, x_n, f_1(x_1, \ldots, x_n), \ldots, f_l(x_1, \ldots, x_n))).$$

It is easy to see that assemblages of the form

$$[(i_1, (t_1/x_1, \ldots, t_n/x_n))] \quad \text{or}$$

$$[(i_1, (t_1/x_1, \ldots, t_n/x_n)); (i_2, (t_1'/x_1, \ldots, t_n'/x_n))] \tag{8.2}$$

(where $i_1 \in \{1, 2\}$, $i_2 \in \{1, 2\}$, and each term t is a variable or has a form $f_j(t_1, \ldots, t_n)$) can be taken as favorable F-assemblages. In this case δ from rule B is equal to 2. Because only two-element assemblages can be generated from two-element assemblages, rule B does not lead us out from the class of assemblages of form (8.2). This class is obviously finite, proving the desired decidability.

In this example a potentially infinite number of possible derivations of formula F was reduced to a finite set of F-assemblages. In more complex situations similar reduction to a finite or infinite decidable set of favorable assemblages is more difficult, but the general schema of the proof is to a large extent unchanged. Many results obtained by this method can be found in [34–36].

8.4   The Formation of Admissible Rules

The formation of admissible rules is one of the most valuable tools used to improve the efficiency of the derivation-search process. This can be seen from results on the acceleration of derivation search for derivation [25, 40], facts from the history of mathematics, and some psychological experiments [41].

Recall that a derivation rule is called admissible in B if adding it to B does not expand the set of objects derivable in B. If all applications of an inference rule can be replaced by a fixed sequence of applications of the initial calculus, then the rule is called *derivable*; derivable rules are a special case of admissible rules. (The sequence of rules—"schema of insertion"— and the number of their applications—"insertion length"—are the same for all applications of a derivable rule.) Other important examples of admissible rules are given by axiom schematas (zero-premise rules generating sets of words trivially derivable in the corresponding calculus). The addition to axioms of some derivable words can be viewed as an analog of introducing zero-premise admissible rules. It is easy to provide examples of admissible rules that are not derivable, such as the cut rule (section 8.2).

EXAMPLE 22 (continued)   The improvement of chess-playing techniques strongly depends on mastering the theory of end games. "Theorems" of this theory (statements such as "The rook will always defeat the king if it is the rook's move") can be taken as axiom schemata of the chess calculus. Some particular "etude mates" can serve to extend this calculus by particular axioms. Sequences of forced moves (for instance, counting exchanges on a given square) can be viewed as an application of a derivable rule. (Exactly in this form, without moving figures mentally and not specifying the order of exchanges, this rule will be used by good chess players.)

EXAMPLE 23 (continued)   The calculus of indefinite integrals can be naturally expanded by theorems of the form "Any rational expression can be integrated in elementary functions." The addition of new axioms corresponds to the expansion of the table of integrals. Recurrent formulas can be viewed as derivable rules. The method of undetermined coefficients can be formulated as an admissible but not derivable rule. It is important to note that the emergence of the integral calculus itself can be considered as the process of developing a new language for the computation of limits of finite sums with powerful admissible rules.

These and many other examples show that the most often emerging admissible rules are derivable or zero-premise rules. This is why the most successful examples of derivation-search methods are related to inventions of proper admissible rules. The most serious improvements of mathematical apparatus, such as the transition from arithmetic to algebra or the development of mathematical analysis, can be naturally described in the same terms. The importance of proper admissible rules is also supported by cut-elimination theorems for logical systems and by theorems that give estimates of the growth of the size of derivations as a result of cut elimination [40].

This suggests two related problems that are important for the development of intelligent systems and for the understanding of the essence of the creative process: the development of proper criteria for the selection of admissible rules and the investigation of mechanisms used to form them. Developing proper criteria is almost identical with the well-known problem of the accumulation of experience, but the formation of admissible rules has not been considered before in sufficiently general form. (Some attempts to state a general form can be found in [42], where the schema of the inverse method is used for the development of admissible rules, such as the combination rule and the end game axiom.) Obviously, both problems are regularly and successfully solved by experts when they develop and improve particular combinatorial algorithms. For this reason I discuss mainly the classification and ordering of the material already in existence in mathematics and programming and the discovery of general principles of orientation in the process of selection. (I do not give recommendations for the practical solution of problems.)

The main mathematical apparatus used for classification is given by the notion of information contained in the given calculus. We compare the information contained in equivalent systems; in other words we compare the different ways used to define the given set of words. It is reasonable to consider a calculus more informative if it has more powerful inference rules, that is, if it generates more words per unit of time. More precisely, an information measure of a calculus B can be given by a function $I(B, n)$ which gives the number of words of length $\leqslant n$ derivable in B.

In this definition we assume that the number of axioms in B is finite and that each derivation in B has a finite number of possible extensions. (This property holds, for example, for canonical calculi.) The computability of $I(B, n)$ requires the decidability of certain properties of B related to the possibility of checking whether a word can be immediately derived by a rule of our calculus. (The property is called the decidability of the corresponding generation basis [43].) We assume this decidability: It holds for practically all calculi (including, of course, canonical systems).

The following statements are obvious:

1. If the number of words derivable in B is finite, then $I(B, n)$ is bounded.
2. If B is deterministic, then $I(B, n) = n$.
3. If each derivation in B has no more than m possible extensions (as, for example, for normal, bounded, shuttle, and other systems), then $I(B, n) \leqslant Cm^n$.

It is easy to show that for any canonical calculus B there is a constant C such that $I(B,n) \leqslant C^{n^2}$. (If the alphabet of B consists of one letter, then $I(B,n) \leqslant C^n$, that is, in this case our estimate is of the same order of magnitude as the one for systems with bounded branching, even though derivations here may have an arbitrary number of continuations.) In all cases it is easy to build a calculus to show that the upper bound can indeed be reached.

It is not difficult to see that the construction of a calculus B' intended to improve the organization of our search should satisfy the following two conditions:

1. The information contents of B should be increased.
2. The number of choices during the search process should be decreased.

These requirements conflict with each other, but only to some extent.

First, even for a given $I(B,n)$ it is possible to decrease the uncertainty of the search procedure by specializing the form of derivations in B (for example, by forbidding certain kinds of derivation). Such a specialization means, in essence, the transition from the initial system B to a new system B'. If B' is equivalent to B, then it is said that the corresponding specialization is admissible. (In the case of search for logical derivation it is customary to talk about tactics and strategies of the search procedure, and the admissibility of the specialization is called the tactic's completeness.) The length of the minimal specialized derivation in the case of admissible specialization does not differ (or differs very little) from the length of the minimal derivation in B. In this case $I(B,n) = I(B',n)$. (If the specialization increases the length of derivations by not more than some additive constant C, then $I(B',n) \leqslant I(B,n+1)$.) At the same time the uncertainty of search can drop significantly (as can be seen from the relation $I(B',p) < I(B,p)$; section 4.2). This is the reason why the investigation of different tactics plays such an important role in the theory of derivation search. (Problems and results on comparison of tactics from [37] can easily be reformulated in informational terms.)

Second, even the most powerful systems can be tectonic, that is, have only one derivation tree for each derivable word.

The main advantage of tectonic and similar systems is almost complete lack of choice during the bottom-up search, that is, a search that starts with the goal word (not the axioms) and moves to possible immediate ancestors of this word. In this way the indeterminacy of search can be reduced to a minimum just by changing the direction of the search. Such a change saves all informational characteristics of the initial calculus. This idea, of course, is broadly used for improving algorithms. For example, the transition to Gentzen's systems without the cut rule is intended for the organization of bottom-up search, and in the inverse method for sequent systems the second change of the direction of search is used. (Search starts with closed assemblages, that is, from "unspecified" axioms that can be used in the proof of the corresponding theorem [36].) Both transitions lead to decreasing the level of indeterminacy of search. It is natural that the new direction of search correspond to the selection process. This problem is considered only for the situation when the direction of search is already fixed. In this case the conflict between the two requirements is especially distinct. To investigate to what degree these two requirements can be reconciled, we consider them individually.

Let us consider different ways in which a system B can be expanded. The simplest possible way is to include all newly generated words in the list of axioms of B. During this process the information $I(p)$ (for a fixed p) may initially increase, but then, necessarily, it will lead to "saturation" and to the subsequent decrease of the information contents. This will not happen, of course, if the list of axioms of B is extended not by all but only by some specially selected words generated in B. In this way the well-known criterion of importance of theorems can be refined: Information is increased more by theorems that generate more new corollaries.

In the discussion we assumed that the new words were added to axioms of B only once, when they were generated for the first time. It is possible to generalize the method used for comparing theorems and eliminate not only repetitions but also "trivial consequences" of generated words. Then we can easily obtain results such as "for inconsistent B, $I(B, p)$ is bounded."

From the practical point of view, the most meaningful statement of the problem of accumulating experience is related (unlike the formulation discussed) to fixing in advance the set of data that can be used to expand B. In this case the cardinality of any possible expansion of B turns out to be bounded by a function p. If such a formulation is chosen, then another well-known criterion of the importance of theorems can be used, namely, "the most important are the short theorems with long proofs." This formulation also supports the contention that it is more effective to expand B by adding new rules to it, not new axioms. Moreover, it is possible to obtain precise results showing that the most effective expansion can be obtained by adding admissible but not derivable rules. Indeed, it is possible to prove that the expansion of B by derivable rules does not change the asymptotic behavior of information [31]. This observation is the main conclusion of this section: The real change in the power of B can be achieved only by adding proper admissible rules to it.

3. Different ways of decreasing the level of indeterminacy of derivation search can be reduced to two ideas: "gluing together" many derivable objects into one and directing the search (which formally can be expressed by a schema of assigning unequal probabilities to different expansions of B). Let us consider the first idea.

Expand the language of our initial system B by "metavariables." Let an object π of the new language serve as a code of set M_π of initial objects. A calculus $\tilde{B}$ in the new language is called a calculus of invariants for B if

$$\forall p\, (p \in B \Rightarrow \exists \pi\, (\pi \in \tilde{B}\, \&\, p \in M_\pi)).$$

If, in addition,

$$\forall \pi\, (\pi \in \tilde{B} \Rightarrow \forall p(p \in M_\pi \Rightarrow p \in B)),$$

then we say that B and $\tilde{B}$ are equivalent in the extended sense.

The calculus $\tilde{B}$ can be, in essence, much more powerful than B but can contain less information indeterminacy. Constructing systems equivalent in the extended sense (in other words, constructing new admissible rules in the language with metavariables) appears to be the most promising method of rationalization of search. Many other facts related to the improvement of methods of solving creative problems can be mentioned to support the effectiveness of the introduction of such admissible rules.

Because it is not always possible to "glue together" derivable objects, it may be useful to introduce the calculus of invariants as an auxiliary measure of improvement of the properties of B.

It is easy to see that the idea of "gluing together" of derivable objects from B agrees completely with the idea of extending B by admissible rules. It is possible to formulate a rule with metavariables in such a way that it will allow a fixed "insertion," but the rules of this type that appear naturally will not be derivable.

It is usually difficult to find a proper way to "glue together" objects of B (even a redundant one as in the calculus of invariants), but there is another always applicable way of decreasing the indeterminacy of search by allowing more freedom in our choice of probabilities. This method also does not contradict increasing the power of the calculus: According to theorem 2 from [31] the level of indeterminacy of the calculus can be minimized for arbitrary initial information $I(p)$. This idea is always used in practice for constructing search algorithms. Strictly, any algorithm transforms the process of search into a deterministic process. But in this case we talk about the probabilities of extensions of incomplete derivations assigned to them a priori (maybe even subconciously) during the design of the corresponding algorithm and used to answer the main question: What extensions should be tried and in what order? This priority of the probabilistic model over the deterministic one can be made even clearer if the search is done mentally.

The objective evaluation of probabilities of possible extensions can be used as a basis for their uneven distribution. This situation is common for games with incomplete information. It can also occur for some games for which information is formally complete. For example, when one tries to compute a forced chess combination, it is easy to overlook a "quiet" response that is considered "highly unlikely." In essence, this last example is located somewhere between computing by assigning probabilities and an arbitrary decision.

One of the advantages of such arbitrary decisions is that it is possible to minimize the indeterminacy (to $\log_2 p$) and to avoid computing the probabilities, when such computation is difficult or simply impossible. This method is broadly used even though its main drawback, the subjectivity of the choice, is obvious. It is enough to mention the algorithm from [44] that is based entirely on such a choice and the well-known method of setting two-sided printed circuits, when one side is used for vertical connections.

A sufficiently general method that leads to an effective selection of the goal can be given by the notion of "fork" in chess.

It should be noted that the mechanism used for selecting a goal (according to the schema of constructing admissible rules of the "combination" type [42]) can be used to form admissible rules, even to form them automatically. The methods that use voluntary decisions concerning the choice of the goal often appear to be some kind of intermediate method that leads eventually to the construction of useful admissible rules (compare with rule B of the inverse method in paragraph 3).

The interplay between the mechanisms of the discrete selection and of the continuous assigning of probabilities is viewed by us as the most adequate model of creative processes. This model can serve as a simplified interpretation of the interaction between the conscious and the subconscious parts of the creative process (where probabilities, as usual, serve as "the refuge for ignorance"). Insight, according to this model, occurs at the moment when the first approximation of the new admissible rule starts to develop. (Often what is realized is not the rule itself but its main idea, the proper domain of metavariables.)

On the other hand, this model differs essentially from the common opposition [46] of the discrete and the continuous, the logical and the geometric in creative thinking. The continuity of the treated objects and the fact that they are three dimensional are only indirectly related to rules by which the objects are handled. The selective and discrete character of the treatment of such objects is seen in this case as clearly as in the case of purely symbolic information. The artificial character of such a distinction is especially clear in the case of proving theorems in graph theory or in the usefulness of "rough" pictures in geometry. There is an interesting question related to our discussion: What is the role of interaction between the left and the right parts of the brain in the process of discovering new admissible rules? What part of the brain is responsible, for example, for the organization of the selection of two-dimensional objects? (The selection of words is known to be done by the left half, but geometric images are thought to be treated by the right half.) The following idea related to the asymmetry of the brain also deserves serious attention: The usefulness for artificial intelligence systems of a special block of "the mythological creativity" [47] corresponding to some features of "right brain" thinking [48]. In our model the unavoidable emergence of incorrect (inadmissible) rules can serve as a sufficiently close analog of this block. (For example, it can be shown that discarding the rules to which small probabilities are assigned can have an arbitrary strong influence on the initial calculus, in particular, incorrect "gluing together" of rules purposely used during the search for invariants of objects derivable in B.)

9 The Asymmetry of Cognitive Mechanisms

The universal character of the notion of a deductive system (or a calculus) allows us to apply the system to the modeling of a variety of discrete processes from different areas of science. Such applications are usually based on the modeling of a particular process by a fixed deductive system and the subsequent investigation of its properties. In more complex situations, however, the nature of a process may require a transition between the various deductive systems. This occurs in applications to the modeling of creative processes, which play a central role in our investigation.

9.1 Two Functions, Two Mechanisms

We start with the investigation of the development process of deductive systems related to improvement of the solution methods for a given class of creative problems. At first glance this program is too narrow a base for our modeling; it seems to be applicable only to certain aspects of the development of mathematics. But this impression is not correct. A number of cognitive processes can be viewed as processes of the search for derivation in the appropriate deductive systems, and hence the construction of such systems and the improvement of methods of search for derivation in them constitute the most important part of the notion of development.

We suggest using a scheme of development of deductive systems that gives causal explanations to a broad set of facts and events. This set will include a large number of cyclical and spiral processes (we refer mainly to historicocultural processes). It will also contain facts pertinent to the functional asymmetry of cerebral hemispheres, which according to our conception reflects the principal difference between two types of cognition, one related to working in a fixed deductive system and the other related to changing it.

A deductive system can be viewed as a method of defining a set. This method consists in specifying initial elements (axioms) of the set as well as specifying inference rules that describe how to generate new elements from the axioms and elements that have already been generated. (Formal grammars give well-known examples of such systems. Numerous other examples can be found [6].)

Given a set M of creative problems, it is often possible to construct a calculus C_M such that its axioms are problems for which solutions are known and its inference rules $S_1,\ldots,S_n \vdash S_0$ guarantee the solvability of problem S_0 if the solutions of $S_1,\ldots,S_n$ are known. A given problem from

M has a solution if and only if it is derivable in C_M. Finding a solution means finding one of the possible derivations in C_M. Thus a calculus provides a "theory" of the given field—a method of fixating the knowledge about the ways to solve problems of a given type that are available at a certain point in time. Accordingly, the process of development of the field consists of stages of two types: work inside a fixed deductive system and the creation and modification of the system itself. (Obviously, the task of dividing a real creative process in these two parts may not be easy.) Because these stages repeatedly give place to each other, a "tower" of calculi comes into being. Its ground floor is occupied by data about the outside world, and transitions between levels are performed on the basis of data produced by systems on the lower levels. Some mathematical details concerning this tower can be found in [8]. This schema is supported by the history of science, but a broader interpretation of terms allows us to apply it to other methods of cognition, the history of spiritual and material cultures, the evolution of individuals and the evolution of society.

Remark 1   To understand the last statement, it is important to realize the level of formalization in our system. Even our initial definition of a deductive system does not require a complete formalization. It may allow some indefiniteness in the description of, say, inference rules. It is easy to see, for instance, that terms such as "the language of culture" and "artistic canon" are similar in many respects to the concept of a calculus. Moreover, various types of indefiniteness can be directly introduced in the language of our calculus. This allows us to have the complete formalization of a syntax while allowing certain degrees of freedom in semantic interpretation. Finally, even if the results of our calculus are completely formalized, the process under investigation—the process of the search for derivation in this calculus—is absolutely informal.

Thus we talk about two different functions of the cognitive process. The first one consists in investigating the current "floor" of the tower, and the second one consists in organization of "advancing to the next floor." This opposition of functions has been described [6] as a conflict between actions directed to the development of the search methods in a fixed calculus and actions directed to its change. These two functions are actually carried out by two cognitive mechanisms.

The clarification of "advancing to the next floor" constitutes an important part of our scheme. It provides a framework for a precise description of transformations that lead to the emergence of the next level calculus and hence allows us to characterize such transformations.

More precisely, we have in mind the reorganization of a deductive system based on including in our language new objects called metavariables (which are used to "glue together" sets of old objects in a new one) and developing "admissible rules" suitable for this new language. (A rule is said to be admissible if it does not expand the set of derivable objects of a given calculus.) The steps in the construction of our tower that allow computer modeling and that require purely human creativity have been described elsewhere [42]. A distinction between the forms of creative thinking that can be mechanized and those that cannot represents one of the most important practical aspects of the opposition of cognitive functions and mechanisms.

Two Mechanisms and the Asymmetry of the Cerebral Hemispheres

The simple schema considered so far suggests that real systems can be divided into two categories: systems that are always located at "a single level" (in other words those that correspond to a single calculus) and more complex systems capable of ascending to the next level. This schema means that any sufficiently complex cognitive system must be able to create new deductive systems. It is obvious that human intellect and the intellect of society as a whole possess this degree of complexity. A society may (at least in principle) realize this ability through an individual, without a special superindividual mechanism. And such an individual will certainly have both necessary mechanisms.

Our point of view is supported by the well-known results on the functional asymmetry of cerebral hemispheres (see, for instance, [48, 51]); these results confirm the concept of functional opposition between the two cognitive mechanisms and help to define the specific characteristics of each. On the basis of these results we will talk about the asymmetry of cognitive mechanisms and call them "left hemisphere" and "right hemisphere" (or simply "left" and "right"; the right hemisphere is responsible for "ascending to the next level").

It is this functional opposition and not its psychophysiological interpretation or the localization of functions in the brain that has a primary character. The asymmetry of the hemispheres probably emerged through the evolutionary process as a realization of this "left"/"right" opposition. In addition, it is important to understand that the phrase "belonging to the right hemisphere," as it is used in this chapter, includes some aspects of the functioning of the subcortex.

Remark 2   While we are on the subject of the biological aspects of "left"/ "right" opposition, we should take into account that, so far as the brain of the modern human is concerned, the mechanism associated with the right hemisphere is more archaic. Roughly, the oldest cognitive mechanism probably materialized through instinctive actions of the body and can be viewed as a form of the "left" mechanism. The capability to develop conditioned reflexes corresponds to the "right" mechanism. Both mechanisms can be found in the animal world. The human brain has an extra, highly developed "left" mechanism capable of unraveling the deductive system that forms the secondary world model. Thus it is the "left" mechanism of secondary modeling that allowed humanity a long stay "on the second level" (recall that the first level contains data about the real world). The "left" mechanism is responsible for singling out humans from the animal world. Moving up to the next level can be done without changing the biological nature of *Homo sapiens*, even though it requires purely creative right-hemisphere types of action.

An analysis of psychological and psychiatric data on the asymmetry of the brain conducted by means of the theory of deductive systems constitutes basis for our conception. Let us summarize the most important oppositions of the "left" and the "right" cognitive mechanisms [32].

1. Local versus global.   The main characteristic of the left-hemisphere way to handle information is its locality. Deriving new information requires a comparatively small amount of already known information (the complexity of an application of a single inference rule is insignificant with respect to the complexity of the whole derivation process). The tendency to split the available information and of considering the obtained parts sequentially is also related to the locality property. On the contrary, the right-hemisphere mechanism is oriented toward global handling of information, toward discovery of those properties that disappear after splitting or partitioning the information. One of the important technical methods of guaranteeing wholeness of perception is parallelism. The psychophysiological content of the local/global opposition is supported by well-known experiments (including the discovery of higher diffusion of excitation in the right hemisphere).

2. Precise objective consideration of possible cases versus approximate

subjective "recognition" (insight).   Objective/subjective opposition (which to a high degree follows from local/global opposition) is characterized by three things. (a) The left-hemisphere search is prolonged in time; insight, on the other hand, most often is a momentary act, separated from the conscious work by a significant amount of time. As a rule, insight is accompanied by a feeling of certainty, and its results can be confirmed easily. In our model insight is related to the recognition of a set as a domain of a metavariable. (b) The probability of making an expedient error in search is negligible, making the "left" cognitive mechanism strive for precision. On the contrary, errors of "insight" are useful and necessary. Thus the "right to make a mistake," imprecision, and the existence of "myths creation block" constitute an important part of the "right" cognitive mechanism. (c) One of the important aspects of left-hemisphere precision is its objectivity. The results of a "left" cognitive process are easily verified and reproduced. It is not difficult to separate them from the subject. Normally, deductive systems satisfy these properties. They can be easily communicated to other people. The "left" mechanism is usually used in the (real or potential) presence of a common language (the left hemisphere is responsible for our language). On the contrary, the "right" cognitive process cannot be separated from the subject until its results are complete (sometimes it cannot be done at all). Right-hemisphere methodology is based on identifying with an object under investigation, whereas left-hemisphere thinking is based on separating subject and object.

3. Consciousness and unconsciousness.   The objectiveness of the "left" cognitive process is due to the conscious character of its actions (etymologically, conscious means common, transferable knowledge). Such consciousness is also necessary to satisfy the high precision requirements. Only the simplest and the shortest sequences of left-hemisphere actions can be executed before their conscious comprehension [32]. On the contrary, such features as parallelism, nondiscreteness [32], and inability to separate subjects from objects make full conscious control over the work of the "right" cognitive process practically impossible. The more detailed analysis of the sphere of unconscious leads to its division into subconscious and superconscious (according to Simonov [52], the superconscious is responsible for forming hypotheses as well as for unselfish motivations). The blending of the activities of sub- and superconsciousness, correlated with the blending of the activity of the subcortex and the cortex, is responsible for a high heterogeneity of right-hemisphere process [32]. This heteroge-

neity seems to be extremely important and deserves further investigation, but it is beyond the boundaries of this chapter.

Modeling "Right" Cognitive Mechanisms

The problem of modeling left-hemisphere activity has been solved, at least in principle. There are many well-developed mathematical models (especially in the framework of the theory of deductive systems and the theory of algorithms). These models are used to develop quality implementations (in the forms of software and hardware), which already far exceed the left-hemisphere ability of even the most talented humans.

At the same time, computers are still far behind humans in the majority of fields requiring intellectual abilities. This lag can be explained by the principal impossibility of constructing working models of the right-hemisphere cognitive mechanism or by our complete lack of expertise in constructing such models.

Of course, there were many attempts to do so. Analog machines, for example, reflect some right-hemisphere features. A sizable part of promising work has been directed toward the development of computers with such right-hemisphere abilities as high level of parallelism and associative memories. In real systems the role of necessary "right-hand" mechanisms is often played by humans engaged in direct dialogue with machines. In theoretical AI work, attempts have been made to simulate right-hemisphere activities by left-hemisphere means. Such attempts, especially in such areas as automated generation of notions, use of analogies, and pattern recognition are quite useful. Various probabilistic approaches as well as the fuzzy sets approach are also of interest. It is obvious, however, that what has been done is not enough, and much more work is needed.

Useful theoretical models of certain features of the "right" cognitive mechanism can be constructed in terms of metavariables and admissible rules. In particular, an interesting example of modeling the local/global opposition can be found in modern methods of search for derivations in logical calculi.

In the method of metavariables (Kanger, Prawitz, Shanin; [12]) we first expand our language by metavariables and then construct an "incomplete inference pattern" in this new language, for which we regularly check whether it is possible to select values of metavariables that will transform this pattern into a real derivation. Almost all the complexity of the method is hidden in one "global" rule of transformation of an "incomplete inference pattern" into an actual derivation. This rule requires a careful correlation between values of metavariables, which is complicated by the fact that a metavariable may occur in different branches of a derivation search tree. The necessity of such an obviously right-hemisphere mental action makes the straightforward computer implementation of the method of metavariables practically impossible. Still the idea can be used effectively in the framework of so-called local methods, such as resolution or inverse methods.

Resolution and inverse methods preserve the main idea—computing only those values of metavariables that are absolutely necessary—and combine it with the local principle of information handling; the complexity of application of inference rules of local methods (resolution rule, rule B, etc.) depends only on the finite number of premises of the rule and not on the derivation as a whole. The feasibility of computer implementations of local methods is based on the suitability of computers for modeling our left-hemisphere mechanism and does not change the fact that the "global" method of metavariables is still the only method that allows us to find the shortest derivation directly by "pure contemplation." If we could find an efficient implementation of global rules, then such a method would be absolutely sufficient. Our discussion shows that the method of metavariables models several important features of the right-hemisphere mechanism. It is also worth mentioning that rule B of the inverse method allows construction of admissible rules with metavariables; that is, it gives an example of a simulation of the right-hemisphere thinking act in the framework of a left-hemisphere local method. We can generalize to the case of reorganization of arbitrary (not necessarily logicomathematical) deductive systems. This generalization also leads to modeling of various features of the right-hemisphere cognitive mechanism. Work in such areas as search for invariants, synthesis of programs from examples, and automatic generation of notions seems to be especially interesting (see [32]).

It is fortunate that a large number of features characteristic for right-hemisphere cognitive process can be modeled in the framework of a comparatively simple and well-investigated propositional logic without making use of complex unsolvable systems such as, say, predicate calculus. But this is probably not surprising: It is no accident that the problem of satisfiability of propositional formulas is called the universal search problem. Now we look at this problem from the point of view of modeling the "right" cognitive process.

9.2 Iterative Methods for Deciding the Satisfiability of Propositional Formulas

The Universal Search Problem

Consider the problem of finding a path through an integer matrix A of the size $3 \times m$ that does not contain zeros or numbers x, y such that $x = -y$. Let n be $\max(\{|x| \mid x \text{ is an element of } A\})$.

An n-vector

$$(x_1, \ldots, x_n) \tag{9.1}$$

of 0's and 1's is called a solution of the problem if there is a path through A containing only i such that $\text{sign}(i) = \text{sign}(x_{[i]} - \frac{1}{2})$. That is, if $x_i = 1$, then the path contains i; otherwise it contains $-i$. This problem can be viewed as a trivial reformulation of the problem of deciding the satisfiability of propositional formulas. (The choice of the number of rows in the matrix A is based on the well-known result that through linear reduction arbitrary propositional formulas can be transformed into formulas in conjunctive normal form with disjunctions consisting of at most three literals.)

For the vector (9.1) it is easy to check (through the number of steps linear with respect to the length of A) if vector (9.1) is a solution of A. At the same time, theoretically 2^n steps are needed to find a solution or to show that it does not exist. This is a typical example of the so-called NP-hard problem, that is, a problem for which considering all possible candidates for solution requires an exponential number of steps, whereas checking whether or not a candidate is indeed a solution can be done in a polynomial number of steps. Moreover, it is possible to prove that this problem is NP-complete, that is, any other NP-hard problem can be reduced to it in polynomial time (see, for instance, [17]). An effective mechanism of generating answers for NP-complete problems could model the most important features of the intuition-based choice process. The actual existence of such a mechanism in our brain would explain many facts that appear to be mysterious in the framework of modern psychology (and sometimes even in the framework of the general paradigm of modern science). That is why it is natural to search for possible realizations of such a mechanism. The model suggested in what follows was decisively influenced by talks by Yu. Matiyasevich and V. Kreynovich presented at a Leningrad seminar on mathematical logic. (Matiyasevich suggested a model based on an electrical circuit composed of superconductive elements that conduct current if and only if there is a path through the corresponding matrix, and Kreynovich related the problem of intuition-based choice to acausal phenomena in physics.)

My model has a "down to earth," left-hemisphere character and can be easily computerized without the use of new technical principles, but it does not guarantee effectiveness of the method. (More precisely, there are theoretical and experimental results that suggest that the method can be effective, but we are still far from an evaluation of complexity for the general case.) The model is especially interesting because it preserves the ability of left-hemisphere cognition and at the same time has almost all characteristics of the right-hemisphere cognitive mechanism. In particular, it reflects the principle of global information processing and realizes parallel handling of an exponential number of paths by a number of processors that depend linearly on the length of the input data.

Another important characteristic of the model is its concordance with contemporary views on neuron organization of the brain. Especially important in this respect are data on the ability of neurons to serve as linear summators and the existence of so-called opponent or reciprocal neurons.

Definition of Iterative Methods

Consider A, m, n as defined in the previous section. For each number i from the set of $2n$ nonzero elements of the matrix A, we define a nonnegative number $d(i)$, called the deferrence of i. The vector

$$(d(-n), d(-n+1), \ldots, d(-1), d(1), \ldots, d(n)) \tag{9.2}$$

is called the obstacle for A. We say that an obstacle defines vector (9.1) if

$$(x_i = 0 \Rightarrow d(-i) = 0) \,\&\, (x_i = 1 \Rightarrow d(i) = 0), \qquad i = 1, \ldots, n.$$

We say that an obstacle is correct if it defines exactly one vector (a correct obstacle contains exactly n zeros). Let us consider an operator $K_{R,L}$ that recalculates the values of deferrence according to the formula

$$d' = R \cdot d(i) + L \cdot \sum_j \min_K \{d(a_{jK})\},$$

where R and L are nonnegative numbers, d' is the new value of deferrence, and j ranges over columns containing $-i$; min is the minimum of all elements of column j except $-i$, and the zeros of the matrix A are deferred by an infinitely large number. $K_{R,L}$ is a uniform, continuous, and piecewise linear operator.

Informally, the new value of deferrence consists of the old value and a characterization of the effort needed for a signal to come through, taking into account previous obstacles and the fact that the signal cannot go through $-i$. It is clear that sometimes it is natural to replace min by other functions (for instance by the arithmetic mean).

LEMMA For any R and L, the space of obstacles defining the solution of the problem A is an invariant space of the operator $K_{R,L}$. (If $R \neq 0$, then the iteration of $K_{R,L}$ preserves the correctness of obstacles defining solutions of A.)

This simple lemma indicates that in many cases the sequence of successive approximations x_n converges in the direction of the solution x. It is important to realize that the direct application of the successive approximation method is often hindered by the fact that the solution is not defined by the main eigendirection of the operator $K_{R,L}$. This can be handled in several different ways. The main method (used also to improve the rate of convergence) is the following: Steps of the application of the operator $K_{R,L}$ alternate with the steps of selection of the completely deferred number (that is, in accordance with some criteria the most deferred of two numbers i and $-i$ is selected and replaced by 0; this corresponds to transforming the corresponding deferrence into 0 and considering only those paths that pass through less deferred numbers). The steps of selection can be carried out periodically (say, once for each k iterations) or can depend on an appearing obstacle (say, when $\max[d(i) - d(-i)]$ crosses over some threshold). The completely deferred number can be selected in accordance with the maximum difference between $d(i)$ and $d(-i)$, by maximal deferrence, or in some other way. At any rate, the definition of a given iterative method consists of specifying R and L, the initial approximation, and the criteria of the applicability of the selection step and of the selection of the deferred number. The description of a particular iterative method and some experimental data about it can be found at the end of this section.

The theoretical investigation of the convergence of iterative methods is still fragmentary and deals only with special classes of matrices. We have sufficient knowledge about the class of $2 \times m$ matrices. (It is known that this class corresponds to the class of polynomial solvability of formulas.) For this class the operator $K_{R,L}$ is linear.

THEOREM Let A be a matrix of dimension $2 \times m$. For any nonzero numbers R, L and for any initial approximation, the sequence of iterations of the operator $K_{R,L}$ directionally converges to an obstacle such that the number maximally deferred by this obstacle can be replaced in A by 0, and the problem of finding a path through a new matrix will still have a solution.

Experiment

The intuitive meaning of the operator $K_{R,L}$ suggests that the strategy of regulating a selection process by k applications of $K_{R,L}$ can be viewed as a certain approximation of the strategy of increasing the freedom of choice previously developed [53]. (The larger k is, the better the approximation). In my experiment on establishing satisfiability, even the simplest approximation (with $k = 1$) proved to be efficient. The experiment deals with the following iterative method: The selection step is used after each application of the operator $K_{0,1}$ to the obstacle consisting of 1's. The number i such that $d(i) > d(-i)$ is selected as a completely deferred number.

Together with this main form of the method, consider two other versions: the auxiliary version (in which the maximally deferred number is completely deferred) and the "reinsurance" version (in which the steps of selection are carried out until the prepondrance of deferrence is greater than 1). If the corresponding selection is impossible, the algorithm will switch to the standard mode (this occurred only in the reinsurance version of the method).

The experiment consisted of two major phases: During the first phase I considered matrices with parameters 3×30 and $n = 7$. (The parameters were selected in the preliminary experiment to obtain matrices with a small number of paths.) Fifty-nine of the sixty-four generated matrices had solutions. In all fifty-nine cases the solutions were found using the main form of the method. The auxiliary method failed to find the correct selection only twice (both times in the last stages of the process). And even in these cases the "reserve of reliability" provided by the "reinsurance" method would prevent us from losing the solutions. The standard (brute force) selection method was not used at all.

During the second phase, I considered matrices corresponding to the problem of coloring Peterson's graphs in three colors [54] and of randomly delimiting their edges [54]. All graphs from $P(5,2)$ to $P(8,5)$ were considered, with delimiting from 0 to β edges from each of these graphs (β is the second parameter of $P(\alpha, \beta)$). The "reinsurance" version reduced each matrix to the two-line form (that is, to the polynomially decidable class) without losing the solvability. The graph $P(43, 13)$, for which the Mints program ([54]; the best one at the time) failed to find the coloring, was considered separately. The "reinsurance" method found the coloring (the method stopped at a satisfiable formula with two three-member columns and 174 two-member columns).

Discussion

A selection step can be viewed as an application of the splitting rule [61] with jumping to one branch. Hence the iterative method algorithm without selection can be viewed as a degenerate case of a selection in the splitting method with priorities assigned to paths. This observation points to the corresponding model of the interaction between hemispheres.

The right-hemisphere mechanism of "absorbing the meaning" of an integral object is modeled by iterations of the operator $K_{R,L}$. In the more favorable cases of direct convergence to an obstacle defining the solution, the effect of "intuitive insight" emerges—unlimited stimulation goes through the path marked by minimal deferrences without experiencing any delay (the short circuit effect). In less favorable cases the recognition is delayed by the necessity of some selection steps (that is, the necessity to involve the left hemisphere). This selection is regulated by preferences accumulated in the corresponding obstacle (that is, during the work of the right-hemisphere mechanism). This division of labor corresponds completely to the model of interaction of hemispheres previously described [31].

The only specific characteristic of the right-hemisphere mechanism (among those already mentioned) that is not reflected in the model is the possibility of the emergence of "intermediate meanings." The problem of validity of propositional formulas (dual to the problem of their satisfiability) is probably more suitable for modeling this characteristic. But such a formulation is closely associated with a difficult mathematical problem known as the equivalence problem for NP and $\overline{\text{NP}}$ classes.

9.3   The Opposition of "Left" and "Right" in Cognition

The material of 9.1 and 9.2 is summarized in table 9.1. I should also point out that the rational perception of one's own activity is typical for the left mechanism, and emotional motivation is typical for the right one. Thus the opposition of reason and emotion is added here. In view of this, important material can be obtained by studying the cognitive possibilities of emotions; these possibilities are definitely close to those of the "right" mechanism in

Table 9.1
Characteristics of cognitive mechanisms

Relative localization in the brain	"Left" mechanism	"Right" mechanism
	Left hemisphere	Right hemisphere, subcortex
Main principle of information processing	Local	Global
Main possibilities	Precise, objective search	Approximate, objective "recognition"
Methodology	Separation of subject and object, analysis	"Identification" with object, synthesis
Kinds of action	Generation by fixed rules, separation	Iterative "delving" into properties of object as a whole
Principle of action	Sequential	Parallel
Results	Accumulation of data, computing answers	Emergence of "meanings," reorganization of calculi
External manifestations	Constructive activity, motion	"Concentrated inaction," immobility
Degree of reflection	Almost complete	Certainly incomplete
Role of time	Unfolding in time	Achronicity

their subjectivity, unconsciousness, nonseparation of reactions, and other features and also by their attraction to subcortical and, generally, more ancient mechanisms. In particular, the interesting experiments described in [55] are in good agreement with this. The experiments demonstrate, for instance, the greater role of emotions in attempts to reorganize existing situations (see [55, p. 87]). Emotional activation gets ahead of the verbalization process, especially in the formation of hypotheses (but not in the evaluation of already existing hypotheses; see [55, pp. 100–104]).

Epistemological Preferences

The approximate recognition of the areas of fruitfulness and of the limits of possibilities of each of the mechanisms, having passed through the emotional component of the person, leads to the formation of distinct epistemological preferences corresponding to the same opposition. Table 9.2 shows the most important of these preferences. It shows, in particular, that the "left" mechanism prefers to dogmatize the laws of the deductive system currently being considered. On the contrary, the "right" mechanism prefers to dogmatize the "given reality" of the phenomenon under consideration while being willful about the system modeling this reality. This

Table 9.2
System of epistemological preferences

"Left" mechanism	"Right" mechanism
Contentment with existing model	Understanding of insufficient adequacy of any model
Positive attitude toward "invented," artificial	Striving for natural, primary
Tendency to schematization, to uncovering "common features"	Attention to individual features deviating from the schema
Deduction	Induction and intuition
Aiming at the future	Achronicity or aiming at the past
Aiming at search for means	Interest in comprehension of goals
Search for truth in dialogue	Individualism of creation

attitude makes it possible to pass to more new adequate calculi. Hence the advantage of the "left" mechanism is the emergence of a new meaningful reality on each level of the tower of deductive systems, and its defect is some degree of dogmatism and the cessation of further ascent. The advantage of the "right" mechanism is the realization of the subordinate role of every particular model ("you shall not make idols"); its typical defect is the tendency to create more and more exquisite interpretations of a single text, closed in itself.

Remark 3 The logic of formation of this system of preferences can be described more precisely in terms of fundamental heuristics ([56]; some mathematical aspects are discussed in [57]). Complexes of such heuristics determine the methodology and epistemology of world views; many pairs of opposing heuristics belong to the same opposition of the "left" and the "right" mechanisms (this is clear from a comparison of table 9.2 with the lists of pairs from [56]). The familiar distinction between rationalism and intuitionism (or, in science, between rationalism and empiricism) also belongs to this opposition.

Analogs of the Asymmetry in General Systems

The functional difference between the "left" and "right" mechanisms has been declared a fundamental quality of the processes of cognition and of development in general; but almost all my observations have to do specifically with the organization of cognition by the human brain. The material so far supports the psychological aspect, rather than the sociological aspect, of the discussion that follows. This argument seems more or less convincing, but it will not hurt to complement it with some arguments from general system theory.

The asymmetry of the mechanisms of grasping reality can influence the process of historical development through not only the individual involved in cognition but also the system qualities of society. I have not attempted to analyze precisely the realization of the "right" and "left" mechanisms in the form of social substructures (such as the "collective subconscious"). I limit myself to a brief discussion of some analogies and possible directions of research.

The basic role belongs here to the familiar opposition of corpuscular (populational) and rigid systems [23]. It is easy to see that the development of corpuscular systems corresponds to "horizontal" motion and that the emergence of a rigid system of the next level on the basis of a corpuscular system corresponds to the function of "ascent." The alternation of both principles of system construction (for instance, in the framework of the same biological organism [23, pp. 16–17]) is in complete correspondence with the emergence of a tower of calculi. The evolutionary aspect of this alternation expresses the important alternate activation of the "left" and "right" mechanisms. This analogy is confirmed by a number of parameters of the opposition of "left" and "right," such as separation/unity, analysis/synthesis, and local/global principles in information processing. (Remember that information is the measure of regularity in the system.)

The opposition of voluntary contractual unities in society and their rigid historical heirs exert strong influence on the historical process; correspondence between this process and the asymmetry discussed is obvious.

Of interest for the discussion of these questions are modifications of the concepts of m-, v-links [58, pp. 100–103], the study of mechanical and other model examples of systems with links of different types, and the results in the theory of algorithms showing that the functioning of a system may slow down "to an arbitrary degree" when links are rigidly fixed (see the violations of the monotonicity condition in [53]).

9.4 The "Left" and the "Right" in Cultures

Two Types of Consciousness

The emotional unity and the unity of the world view characteristic of the "left" and "right" complexes allow us to speak of two types of consciousness, each affecting not only cognitive processes but also the totality of manifestations of human personality, the formation of tastes and preferences in different areas of culture and society. We will see how this influence affects the stylistic coloring of most historical and cultural phenomena. We will clearly see the periods of the alternating domination of one or the other type of consciousness in society.

Remark 4   Along with the "pure" periods, there exist, of course, transitional ones. This "purity" is itself relative, and, generally, every significant phenomenon shows to some degree a combination of "left" and "right" features. Any scheme, when applied to such an intricate phenomenon as culture, looks too crude; still it may be useful and even have some prognostic power.

The general reasons for the alternation of "left" and "right" domination are sufficiently clear: They follow from the obvious limitedness of each of the cognitive mechanisms and from the obvious incompatibility of some aspects of their work. Despite the existing attraction of individuals, societies, and cultures toward one type of consciousness, problems arise that some time or other make it necessary to activate the opposing mechanism. The only exceptions are pathological cases (in the medical sense) and dead ends in the history of culture. The change of the dominating type of consciousness manifests itself in disappointment in the ideas and culture of the previous period; the typical length of this period often shows that effect is directly connected with the problem of "fathers and sons."

This concept does not assume, for instance, the existence of a larger number of "right hemispherists" in the physiological sense in the period of the domination of the "right" complex in society. We can think only of the existence of better conditions for social advancement for them.

The analysis of the features of the "left" and "right" types of consciousness is performed on the basis of the oppositions shown in tables 9.1 and 9.2, plus the opposition of *optimism* and *pessimism*. Experimental data show that the disconnection of the right hemisphere leads to euphoria, whereas the disconnection of the left hemisphere leads to depression. Each step of the "left" activity is possible without overcoming significant difficulties, which naturally brings satisfaction; this satisfaction can be marred only by the "right" feeling that the actions are meaningless. On the contrary, the "right" work of "ascent" is much more difficult; it has no guarantee of success or criteria of its closeness, and it can very well lead to the emotions taking part in the formation of an inferiority complex. (Such emotions necessarily emerge when the left hemisphere is suppressed, so that goals remain but the means needed to achieve them are lost). Short periods of enthusiasm separated by long periods of depression appear to be rather typical for the emotional coloring of the work of the "right" mechanism. In combination with the orientation of "left" toward the future and of "right" toward the past and a number of other considerations, this suggests that optimism is characteristic for the "left" consciousness and pessimism for the "right" one.

Artistic Styles

Futurism is related to the optimism of the left hemisphere and to its love of the artificial; pragmatism is related to its constructivity; functionality is related to its "following the laws of reason." More precisely, reason may, in fact, be the dogmatization of the existing model, which necessarily leads to pseudofunctionality. Beauty is understood here as high expediency, and freedom as recognized necessity. Formed in a similar way is the complex of "right" consciousness, with its pessimism, orientation toward the past, escapism, antipragmatism, romantic willfulness, and the understanding of beauty as the result of free and painful creative effort.

I take architecture as the main example. Typical for "left" architectural styles are strict and logical structures, aiming at the "honest" display of the construction, etc. A "right" style is characterized, on the contrary, by sensuality, tendency to fancifulness, and grotesque, aggravated decor and pretentiousness, seeking to conceal the construction. It is natural to call the "left" architectural styles classical and the "right" styles baroque. Examples are given in table 9.3. Particular styles possess "left" and "right"

Table 9.3
Styles of the sixteenth through twentieth centuries

Classical "left" styles	Baroque "right" styles
High Renaissance	Mannerism
Palladian style	Baroque
Classicism	–
Empire style	Rococo
Engineer style	Romanticism, eclecticism
Constructivism	Modern
The style of the 1950s through 1960s	Retrospective style

features to different degrees. They coexist and replace each other in various ways, but the alternation of dominating tendencies is manifested rather distinctly.

"Social Styles"

"Left" pragmatism and reliance on reason are connected to the tendency to calculate and to the formal and judicial foundations of society. The "left" is associated with urbanism, interest in technology, scientism, the spirit of compromise, and reformism (attempts to reconstruct life gradually on the basis of a contract in a reasonable way). Opposing this is the "recklessness" of "right" consciousness, its aversion to formalism, and its desire to simplify and to go back to nature. Both maximalism and political conservatism exhibit "right" consciousness (conservatism, that is, respect for traditions and the "organic foundations of authority," has features of "right" dogmatism and should not be mistaken for the "left" dogmatization of a model).

The "left" is aimed at common knowledge and linguistic interaction. The "right" complex includes respect for the intuitive, instinctive, and ineffable ("an uttered thought is a lie"). This leads to a greater spiritual concentration and reserve and sometimes to larger approximateness ("if one cannot be precise ...," "if one cannot be a saint, why be honest"). An important parameter of this distinction is the opposition of openness to separatism. On the same axis we find the oppositions of cosmopolitanism and nationalism, of Westernizers and Slavophiles.

The "right" maximalism is the point where the "right" and "left" extremists in the usual political sense of these words meet each other. Among the components of revolutionary process one can find reformism and the desire to organize the society in a reasonable way on the one hand, and maximalism and romanticism on the other. Victorious revolutions (as well as the revolutions that are exhausted when most of its demands are satisfied) exhibit the preponderance of the "left" consciousness in society. On the contrary, suppressed revolts that result in the deterioration of the situation of the insurgents show the preponderance of the "right."

The "right" is infested with distrusting reason; the "left" with trusting it too much. The advantage of the "left" is its constructivity; its frequent defects are shallowness and groundlessness. The "right" can be deeper but is often unable and unwilling to act, to create civilization. Goncharov's *Stolz*, possibly, does not allow mankind to cease acting, whereas *Oblomov* prevents it from losing the meaning of activity.

Artistic Styles and the State of Society

The existence of correlation between the state of society and the art created
in it has been discussed in the literature many times. But, to the best of my
knowledge, the form of this correlation based on "left"/"right" opposition
has never been proposed with sufficient definiteness. Briefly, this form can
be expressed by saying that liberalism corresponds to classicism and dicta-
torship to baroque. More precisely, classical styles are superimposed on
"left" periods, baroque-type styles on "right" periods, whereas the periods
with a clearly expressed combination of "left" and "right" tendencies in
politics often show the coexistence of classical and baroque-type elements
in architecture (late Renaissaince, baroque of Peter the Great, the late stage
of Russian modernism, etc.). The superposition usually occurs with the
precision of up to five years. I illustrate it here with the example of architecture because architecture is a form of art that is more dependent on social
conditions than other art forms.

It is important to point out that this correlation has a geographical
aspect. For instance, Italy, Spain, and Germany, going through the "second
edition of serfdom," spent much more time in a "baroque" state after 1500
than England, France, and Holland. As another example, I can mention
the simplicity and severity of the architecture of Novgorod and Pskov and
a similar tendency in the northern provinces of Russia, where serfdom was
almost nonexistent. A third example: After the Netherlands Revolution, the
northern states became independent, whereas the southern states remained
a part of the stagnant Spanish monarchy; the culture, which had been
homogeneous until then, split, with classicism triumphing in the north and
baroque in the south. Compare also the definite attraction of the famous
East/West opposition to the "left"/"right" opposition.

By definition, the type of a period is often revealed only by its results.
Therefore there exist even possibilities of predicting the historical process
by the artistic state of the epoch. For instance, by looking at the architecture
of Inigo Jones, one could have predicted the victory of the English and
French revolutions. It is important here to note that artistic changes often
happen before social ones. At this point my theory sharply differs from the
so-called "vulgar sociological" ones.

From this point of view, I have studied in great detail the data on the
history of Russia and a number of countries of Western Europe in the sixteenth through eighteenth centuries. The shortest of the complete periods

uncovered in this study constituted fifty to eighty years. A number of changes took place synchronously in different countries, which demonstrates the interconnectedness of their cultures. For instance, the "left" period of 1565–1570 in Western Europe constrasts with the "right" period in Russia, but 200 years later the European "left" period and classicism grip Russia.

References

[1] Post, E. L. 1943. "Formal reduction of the general combinatorial decision problem." *American Journal of Mathematics* 65(2): 197–215.

[2] Bertalanffy, L. von, 1968. *General System Theory: Foundations, Development, Applications.* New York: George Braziller.

[3] Wiener, N. 1956. *I Am a Mathematician.* Cambridge, Mass.: MIT Press.

[4] Novikov, P. S. 1964. *Elements of Mathematical Logic.* Edinburgh: Oliver and Boyd.

[5] Mendelson, E. 1964. *Introduction to Mathematical Logic.* New York: Van Nostrand.

[6] Yudin, D. B., and Goldstein, E. G. 1964. *Problems and Methods of Linear Programming* (in Russian). Moscow: Sovetskoye Radio.

[7] Berdichevsky, D. D., and Marchenko, V. A. 1978. *The Automated Design of Ship Cable Nets* (in Russian). Leningrad: Sudostroyeniye.

[8] Gaaze-Rapoport, M. G., Pospelov, D. A., and Semyonova, E. T. 1980. *The Generation of Structures of Fairy Tales* (in Russian). Moscow: Nauchny Sovet po Kompleksnoy Probleme Kibernetika.

[9] Gladky, A. V., and Melchuk, I. A. 1969. *Elements of Mathematical Linguistics* (in Russian). Moscow: Nauka.

[10] Aho, A. and Ullman, J. 1972. *The Theory of Parsing, Translation and Compiling.* Englewood Cliffs, N.J.: Prentice Hall.

[11] Manin, Yu. I. 1980. *The Computable and the Noncomputable* (in Russian). Moscow: Sovetskoye Radio.

[12] Markov, A. A. 1961. *Theory of Algorithms.* Jerusalem: Israel Program for Scientific Translation.

[13] Kleene, S. C. 1952. *Introduction to Metamathematics.* New York: Van Nostrand.

[14] Maslov, S. Yu. 1964. "Some properties of the apparatus of canonical calculi" (in Russian). *Proceedings of the Steklov Institute of Mathematics* 72: 5–56.

[15] Smyllian, R. 1961. "Extended canonical systems." *Proceedings of the American Mathematical Society* 12(3): 440–442.

[16] Trakhtenbrot, B. A. 1963. *Algorithms and Automatic Computing Machines.* Boston: Heath.

[17] Aho, A., Hopcroft, J., and Ullman, J. 1974. *Design and Analysis of Computer Algorithms.* Reading, Mass.: Addison-Wesley.

[18] Iaglom, A. M., and Iaglom, I. M., 1983. *Probability and Information* Boston: Reidel.

[19] Gnedenko, B. V., and Khinchin, A. Ya. 1961. *An Elementary Introduction to the Theory of Probability.* San Francisco: Freeman.

[20] Maslov, S. Yu., and Rusakov, E. D. 1976. "Probabilistic canonical calculi." *Journal of Soviet Mathematics* 6(1): 401–409.

[21] Syroezhin, I., ed. 1974. *Cybernetics in Economics: Foundations of the Theory of Economic Systems* (in Russian). Leningrad: LGU.

[22] Bergson, H. 1911. *Creative Evolution.* New York: Holt.

[23] Anonymous. 1970. "The system approach in modern biology," in *System Studies* (in Russian). Moscow: Nauka.

[24] Kac, M. 1959. *Probability and Related Topics in Physical Sciences.* London and New York: Interscience Publishers.

[25] Maslov, S. Yu. 1976. "Deduction search in calculi of general type." *Journal of Soviet Mathematics* 6(1): 395–400.

[26] Orevkov, V. P. 1983. "The British Museum algorithm can be more efficient than the resolution method," in the Russian translation of *Symbolic Logic and Mechanical Theorem Proving*, C.-L. Chang and R. C.-T. Lee, eds. Moscow: Nauka, 314–332.

[27] Norgela, S. A. 1974. "The growth of derivations caused by the introduction of minus-normality," in *The Theory of Logical Deduction* (in Russian). Moscow: Nauka, vol. 1.

[28] Maslov, S. Yu., and Norgela, S. A. 1977. "Cut-type rules in calculi of general type." *Journal of Soviet Mathematics* 8(3): 289–298.

[29] Kanger, S. 1963. "A simplified proof method for elementary logic," in *Computer Programming and Formal Systems*, P. Braffort and D. Hirschberg, eds. Amsterdam: North-Holland, 87–93.

[30] Chang, C.-L., and Lee, R. C.-T. 1973. *Symbolic Logic and Mechanical Theorem Proving.* New York: Academic Press.

[31] Maslov, S. Yu. 1979. "Information in a calculus and the rationalization of search" (in Russian). *Kibernetika* 2: 20–26.

[32] Maslov, S. Yu. 1979. "The theory of derivation search and the problems of the psychology of creativity" (in Russian). *Semiotika i Informatika* 13: 17–46.

[33] Maslov, S. Yu. 1964. "An inverse method of establishing deducibilities in the classical predicate calculus." *Soviet Mathematics, Doklady* 5: 1420–1423.

[34] Maslov, S. Yu. 1966. "Application of the inverse method of establishing deducibility to the theory of decidable fragments of the classical predicate calculus." *Soviet Mathematics, Doklady* 7: 1653–1657.

[35] Maslov, S. Yu. 1969. "Invertible sequential variant of constructive predicate calculus," in *Seminars in Mathematics* 4. New York and London: Steklov Institute of Mathematics, Consultants Bureau, 36–42.

[36] Maslov, S. Yu. 1971. "The inverse method for establishing deducibility in logical calculi." *Proceedings of the Steklov Institute of Mathematics* 98: 25–96.

[37] Maslov, S. Yu. 1971. "Relationship between tactics of the inverse method and the resolution method," in *Seminars in Mathematics* 16. New York and London: Steklov Institute of Mathematics, Consultants Bureau, 69—73.

[38] Maslov, S. Yu. 1971. "Proof-search strategies for methods of the resolution type," in *Machine Intelligence*, B. Meltzer and D. Michie, eds. New York: American Elsevier, vol. 6, 77–90.

[39] Davydov, G. V., Maslov, S. Yu., Mints, G. E., Orevkov, V. P., and Slisenko, A. O. 1971. "A machine algorithm for establishing deducibility on the basis of the inverse method," in *Seminars in Mathematics* 16. New York and London: Steklov Institute of Mathematics, Consultants Bureau, 1–6.

[40] Tseytin, G. S. 1971. "On the complexity of derivation in propositional calculus," in *Seminars in Mathematics* 8. New York and London: Institute of Mathematics, Consultants Bureau, 115–125.

[41] Pushkin, V. N. 1967. *Heuristics: The Science about Creative Thought* (in Russian). Moscow: Politizdat.

[42] Maslov, S. Yu. 1972. "Derivation search as a model of the heuristic process" (in Russian). *Kybernetika* 5: 74–78.

[43] Maslov, S. Yu. 1967. "The concept of strict representability in the general theory of calculi." *Proceedings of the Steklov Institute of Mathematics* 93: 1–50.

[44] Botvinnik, M. V. 1975. *On the Cybernetical Goal of a Chess Game* (in Russian). Moscow: Sovetskoye Radio.

[45] Maslov, S. Yu. 1978. "Macroevolution as a deduction process." *Synthese* 39: 417–434.

[46] Birkhoff, G. 1977. *Mathematics and Psychology* (in Russian). Moscow: Sovetskoye Radio.

[47] Lotman, Yu. M. 1977. *Culture as Collective Intelligence and Problems of Artificial Intelligence* (in Russian). Moscow: Nauchny Sovet po Kompleksnoy Probleme Kibernetika.

[48] Ivanov, V. V. 1978. *Even and Odd* (in Russian). Moscow: Sovetskoye Radio.

[49] Maslov, S. Yu. 1975. "Mutation calculi," *Journal of Soviet Mathematics* 10(4): 496–517.

[50] Maslov, S. Yu. 1975. "Theory of derivation search and its applications" (in Russian). *Kibernetika* 4: 134–144.

[51] Balonov, L. Ya., and Deglin, V. L. 1976. *Hearing and Speech of the Dominant and the Nondominant Hemispheres* (in Russian). Leningrad: Nauka.

[52] Simonov, P. V. 1978. *The Classification of the Conscious, Subconscious and Superconscious* (in Russian). Tbilisi: Metsniyeroba.

[53] Maslov, S. Yu. 1979. "Calculi with monotone deductions and their economic interpretation," *Journal of Soviet Mathematics* 20(4): 2314–2321.

[54] Mints, G. E. 1978. "A program for refuting propositional formulas," in *Artificial Intelligence and the Automation of Research* (in Russian). Kiev: Naukova Dumka.

[55] Vasilev, I. A., Popluzhny, V. L., and Tikhomirov, O. K. 1968. *Emotions and Thought* (in Russian). Moscow: MGU.

[56] Maslov, S. Yu. 1976. "Analysis of areas of applicability of fundamental heuristics" (in Russian), in *Seventh Symposium on Logic and Methodology of Science*. Kiev: Naukova Dumka.

[57] Maslov, S. Yu. 1974. "Possibilities of application of the theory of deductive systems" (in Russian), in *The Theory of Logical Deduction*, Moscow: Nauka, vol. 1.

[58] Anonymous. 1970. *The Modeling of Social Processes* (in Russian). Moscow: Nauka.

[59] Noether, G. E. 1967. *Elements of Nonparametric Statistics*. New York: Wiley.

[60] Galil, Z. 1976. "On enumeration procedures for theorem proving and for integer programming," in *Automata, Languages and Programming*, S. Michaelson and R. Milner, eds. Edinburgh: University Press.

[61] Maslov, S. Yu., and Dantsin, E. Ya. 1980. "The splitting method and other systems," in *Methods of Mathematical Logic in Problems of Artificial Intelligence, Abstracts of Papers and Communications* (in Russian). Vilnus.

The MIT Press, with Peter Denning as consulting editor, publishes computer science books in the following series:

ACM Doctoral Dissertation Award and Distinguished Dissertation Series

Artificial Intelligence, Patrick Winston and Michael Brady, editors

Charles Babbage Institute Reprint Series for the History of Computing, Martin Campbell-Kelly, editor

Computer Systems, Herb Schwetman, editor

Foundations of Computing, Michael Garey, editor

History of Computing, I. Bernard Cohen and William Aspray, editors

Information Systems, Michael Lesk, editor

Logic Programming, Ehud Shapiro, editor

The MIT Electrical Engineering and Computer Science Series

Scientific Computation, Dennis Gannon, editor